Explore THE UNITED STATES

History

History is the story of people and places from the past.

Welcome to

Kitsap Peninsula

in Washington

Pacific Northwest Native Americans used cedar trees to build **shelters,** or homes. They also carved huge canoes from cedar trees.

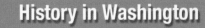

Kitsap
Peninsula

Fast Fact:
Some canoes were almost 50 feet long and could hold 20 people.

Native Americans still carve canoes, as did their ancestors. An **ancestor** is a member of your family who lived long ago.

Link to You
How could you learn about one of your ancestors?

E3

Economics

Economics is the study of how money, goods, and services are made and used.

Welcome to the Bootheel

Youth

Museum

in Malden, Missouri

You can learn about many jobs at the museum. A **job** is work that people do. People may get money for doing a job.

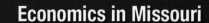

Malden

You can learn about banks at the museum. A bank is where people save money. **Save** means to keep.

Fast Fact:

Long ago, people used shells, beads, feathers, and stones as money.

You can get play money from the museum's bank to use at the grocery store. You can use the money at the store's play cash register!

NOT LEGAL TENDER

Link to You

What are three jobs that you do?

E5

Science and Technology

**Science and Technology change
the way we live.**

Welcome to the Kennedy
SP★CE
CENTER
in Titusville, Florida

Space shuttles lift off from Kennedy
Space Center. Rockets help get the
shuttles into space. Astronauts learn
about space. They communicate
what they learn to scientists on
Earth. **Communicate** means to
tell about something.

*A space shuttle
lifts off.*

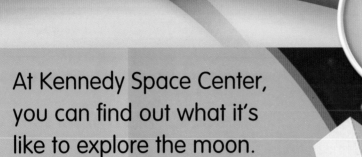

Titusville

At Kennedy Space Center, you can find out what it's like to explore the moon. **Explore** means to go to new places and to learn about them.

Fast Fact:

A spacesuit makes it possible for astronauts to breathe, stay warm, walk, talk, and see into dark places!

Link to You

Tell about places you would like to explore.

E7

Geography

Geography is the study of the Earth and the way people use it.

Welcome to Mackinac Island, Michigan

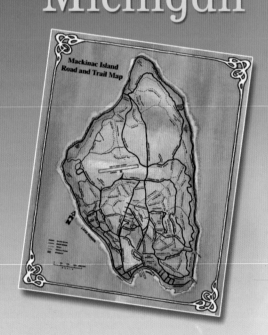

Mackinac Island
Road and Trail Map

A **map** is a drawing of a place. This is a map of Mackinac Island. An **island** is land with water all around it.

Arch Rock is a natural rock bridge. Water wore away the middle of the rock!

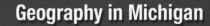

Mackinac
Island

Fast Fact:

Arch Rock is about 150 feet tall—almost as tall as an eleven story building!

There are no cars on Mackinac Island. People walk, use horses, or ride bicycles for transportation. **Transportation** is a way of moving people or goods from place to place.

Link to You

Tell about transportation where you live. How is it like or different from Mackinac Island?

E9

Culture

Culture is the way a group of people lives.

Welcome to the Classical Chinese Garden

in Portland, Oregon

It is a tradition for Chinese gardens to have plants, water, stones, and garden buildings. A **tradition** is the way something has been done for a long time.

Portland

Visitors can sit and sip tea at the tea house in the garden.

Fast Fact:

In China, gardening is a form of art, just like painting and drawing.

People celebrate Chinese New Year at the garden. Chinese New Year is a **holiday,** or special day. The lion dance is a tradition on this holiday.

Link to You

Tell about your favorite holiday. What traditions do you have on that day?

Citizenship

Citizenship is being a good member of a nation or community.

Welcome to Bristol, Rhode Island

The birthday of our country is on July 4. We show pride for our country on this day. **Pride** means to feel good about something.

Red, white, and blue stripes are painted down the streets of Bristol all year long.

Bristol

Citizens respect the flag. **Respect** means to treat something in a special way.

Citizens in Bristol work together to make the floats for the July 4 parade.

THE SPIRIT OF AMERICA

Fast Fact:

Bristol has the oldest July 4 celebration in our country.

Link to You

A good citizen treats others with respect. How do you show respect for people?

Government

Government is a group of people who work together to run a city, state, or country.

Welcome to the

Arizona
Capitol Museum
in Phoenix, Arizona

A **capitol** is a building where people meet to make laws. Long ago, the Capitol Museum building was used by lawmakers for meetings.

Phoenix ★

Each state has a leader called a governor. Citizens of each state vote for their governor. A **citizen** is a member of a state and country.

Arizona Governor
Janet Napolitano

The Arizona State Seal is on the floor of the Capitol Museum.

Fast Fact:

The Capitol Museum has a lifelike wax figure of the State of Arizona's first governor, George Wiley Paul Hunt.

Link to You

How does government help people?

National Symbols

United States Flag

◀ The flag of the United States is red, white, and blue. It is a symbol of our country.

Harriet Tubman

Black Heritage USA 13c

© 1978 USPS.

U.S. Stamp

▲

Some U.S. stamps show important Americans. These stamps are a symbol of honor for the different people who have made our country great.

Statue of Liberty

▲

The Statue of Liberty is a very tall statue in New York Harbor. It is a symbol of hope and freedom.

SCOTT FORESMAN

SOCIAL STUDIES

ALL TOGETHER

PROGRAM AUTHORS

Dr. Candy Dawson Boyd
Professor, School of Education
Director of Reading Programs
St. Mary's College
Moraga, California

Dr. Geneva Gay
Professor of Education
University of Washington
Seattle, Washington

Rita Geiger
Director of Social Studies and
Foreign Languages
Norman Public Schools
Norman, Oklahoma

Dr. James B. Kracht
Associate Dean for Undergraduate
Programs and Teacher Education
College of Education
Texas A&M University
College Station, Texas

Dr. Valerie Ooka Pang
Professor of Teacher Education
San Diego State University
San Diego, California

Dr. C. Frederick Risinger
Director, Professional Development
and Social Studies Education
Indiana University
Bloomington, Indiana

Sara Miranda Sanchez
Elementary and Early Childhood
Curriculum Coordinator
Albuquerque Public Schools
Albuquerque, New Mexico

CONTRIBUTING AUTHORS

Dr. Carol Berkin
Professor of History
Baruch College and the Graduate Center
The City University of New York
New York, New York

Lee A. Chase
Staff Development Specialist
Chesterfield County Public Schools
Chesterfield County, Virginia

Dr. Jim Cummins
Professor of Curriculum
Ontario Institute for Studies in Education
University of Toronto
Toronto, Canada

Dr. Allen D. Glenn
Professor and Dean Emeritus
Curriculum and Instruction
College of Education
University of Washington
Seattle, Washington

Dr. Carole L. Hahn
Professor, Educational Studies
Emory University
Atlanta, Georgia

Dr. M. Gail Hickey
Professor of Education
Indiana University-Purdue University
Fort Wayne, Indiana

Dr. Bonnie Meszaros
Associate Director
Center for Economic Education and
Entrepreneurship
University of Delaware
Newark, Delaware

CONTENT CONSULTANTS

Catherine Deans-Barrett
World History Specialist
Northbrook, Illinois

Dr. Michael Frassetto
Studies in Religions
Independent Scholar
Chicago, Illinois

Dr. Gerald Greenfield
Hispanic-Latino Studies
History Department
University of Wisconsin, Parkside
Kenosha, Wisconsin

Dr. Frederick Hoxie
Native American Studies
University of Illinois
Champaign, Illinois

Dr. Cheryl Johnson-Odim
Dean of Liberal Arts and Sciences and
Professor of History
African American History Specialist
Columbia College
Chicago, Illinois

Dr. Michael Khodarkovsky
Eastern European Studies
University of Chicago
Chicago, Illinois

Robert Moffet
U.S. History Specialist
Northbrook, Illinois

Dr. Ralph Nichols
East Asian History
University of Chicago
Chicago, Illinois

CLASSROOM REVIEWERS

Diana Vicknair Ard
Woodlake Elementary School
St. Tammany Parish
Mandeville, Louisiana

Sharon Berenson
Freehold Learning Center
Freehold, New Jersey

Betsy Blandford
Pocahontas Elementary School
Powhatan, Virginia

Nancy Neff Burgess
Upshur County Schools
Buckhannon-Upshur Middle School
Upshur County, West Virginia

Gloria Cantatore
Public School #5
West New York, New Jersey

Stephen Corsini
Content Specialist in Elementary Social Studies
School District 5 of Lexington
and Richland Counties
Ballentine, South Carolina

Deanna Crews
Millbrook Middle School
Elmore County
Millbrook, Alabama

LuAnn Curran
Westgate Elementary School
St. Petersburg, Florida

Kevin L. Curry
Social Studies Curriculum Chair
Hickory Flat Elementary School
Henry County, McDonough, Georgia

Sheila A. Czech
Sky Oaks Elementary School
Burnsville, Minnesota

Louis De Angelo
Office of Catholic Education
Archdiocese of Philadelphia
Philadelphia, Pennsylvania

Dr. Trish Dolasinski
Paradise Valley School District
Arrowhead Elementary School
Glendale, Arizona

Dr. John R. Doyle
Director of Social Studies Curriculum
Miami-Dade County Schools
Miami, Florida

Dr. Roceal Duke
District of Columbia Public Schools
Washington, D.C.

Peggy Flanagan
Roosevelt Elementary School
Community Consolidated School District #64
Park Ridge, Illinois

Mary Flynn
Arrowhead Elementary School
Glendale, Arizona

Odaly Garcia
Claude Pepper Elementary School
Miami, Florida

Su Hickenbottom
Totem Falls Elementary School
Snohomish School District
Snohomish, Washington

Allan Jones
North Branch Public Schools
North Branch, Minnesota

Ruth Rae Koth
Pinellas County
Bear Creek Elementary School
St. Petersburg, Florida

Martha Sutton Maple
Shreve Island School
Shreveport, Louisiana

Lyn Metzger
Carpenter Elementary School
Community Consolidated School District #64
Park Ridge, Illinois

Marsha Munsey
Riverbend Elementary School
West Monroe, Louisiana

Christine Nixon
Warrington Elementary School
Escambia County School District
Pensacola, Florida

Cynthia K. Reneau
Muscogee County School District
Columbus, Georgia

Brandon Dale Rice
Secondary Education Social Science
Mobile County Public School System
Mobile, Alabama

Liz Salinas
Supervisor
Edgewood ISD
San Antonio, Texas

Beverly Scaling
Desert Hills Elementary
Las Cruces, New Mexico

Madeleine Schmitt
St. Louis Public Schools
St. Louis, Missouri

Barbara Schwartz
Central Square Intermediate School
Central Square, New York

Editorial Offices:
• Glenview, Illinois
• Parsippany, New Jersey
• New York, New York

Sales Offices:
• Parsippany, New Jersey
• Duluth, Georgia
• Glenview, Illinois
• Coppell, Texas
• Ontario, California
• Mesa, Arizona

www.sfsocialstudies.com

ISBN: 0-328-07568-X

Contents

Social Studies Handbook

UNIT 1

Time for School

In My Community

UNIT 3

Work! Work! Work!

UNIT 4

Our Earth, Our Resources

UNIT 6

Our Country, Our World

Reference Guide

Social Studies Handbook

Biographies

Maps

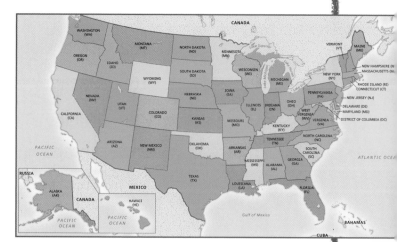

Skills

Citizenship Skills

There are many ways to show good citizenship. In your textbook, you will learn about people who are good citizens in their community, state, and country.

Respect means treating others as you want to be treated.

Caring means thinking about how someone feels and doing something to show you care.

Responsibility means doing the things you should do.

Fairness
means taking turns and playing by the rules.

Honesty
means telling the truth.

Courage
means doing what is right even when it is hard.

★ Citizenship in Action ★

Good citizens make careful decisions. They learn to solve problems. Help these children act like good citizens. Here are the steps they follow.

Problem Solving

The Art Center is messy. What can they do?

1. Name the problem.
2. Find out more about the problem.
3. List ways to solve the problem.
4. Talk about the best way to solve the problem.
5. Solve the problem.
6. How well is the problem solved?

★ Citizenship in Action ★

Decision Making

Open House is tonight. The children want to make a sign to welcome their parents.

1. Tell what decision you need to make.

2. Gather information.

3. List your choices.

4. Tell what might happen with each choice.

5. Make a decision.

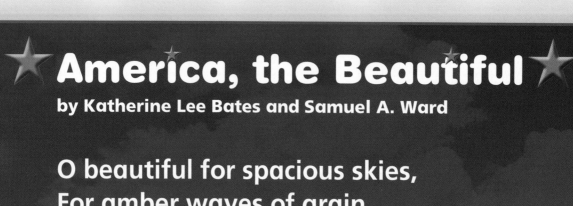

America, the Beautiful

by Katherine Lee Bates and Samuel A. Ward

O beautiful for spacious skies,
For amber waves of grain,
For purple mountains majesties
Above the fruited plain!
America! America!
God shed his grace on thee,
And crown thy good with brotherhood
From sea to shining sea!

The White House

The Lincoln Memorial

The Jefferson Memorial

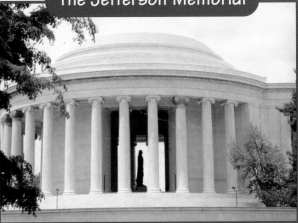

Citizenship Skills

Mount Rushmore

Statue of Liberty

Vietnam Veterans Memorial

Flag Rules

You should follow these rules when you say the Pledge of Allegiance.

1. First, you should stand.
2. Then, you should face the flag
3. Next, you should put your right hand over your heart. This shows honor and respect
4. Last, you should say the Pledge of Allegiance!

The Pledge of Allegiance

I pledge allegiance to the Flag of the United States of America, and to the Republic for which it stands, one Nation under God, indivisible, with liberty and justice for all.

Living History from

Colonial Williamsburg
www.history.org

Think Like a Historian

Some people who study history carefully dig for objects in the ground.

Many things they find are broken. This plate is broken. It must be put back together to see what it looks like.

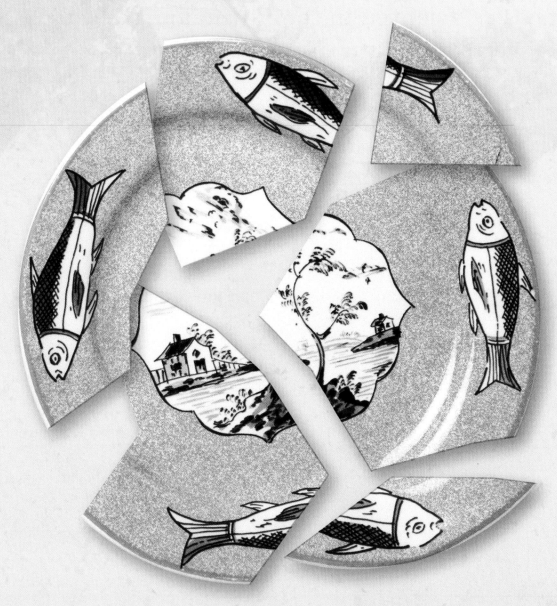

What did this plate look like when it was new? Draw a picture. Show what it may have looked like.

H11

Find the Facts

Suppose a scientist in the future found these objects buried in the ground. Scientists ask questions to learn more about things. Look at some of the questions they ask. How would you answer these questions?

1 What are the objects?

2 Who used the objects?

3 Why did people use them?

4 How did people use them?

5 When did people use them?

6 Where did people use them?

Use Different Resources

There are many different resources you can use to get information. Colonial Williamsburg is in Virginia. Suppose you want to learn more about the state of Virginia.

Encyclopedia

An encyclopedia has information about many topics. The topics are in alphabetical order. You can find out more about Virginia by looking under "V" in the encyclopedia.

Dictionary

A dictionary lists words in alphabetical order. It tells what words mean. It also shows you how to spell and say words. Where in the dictionary would you look to find out how to say *Virginia*?

Atlas

An atlas is a book of maps. An atlas of the United States will show you where Virginia is.

Internet

The Internet is a system of computers that store information. You could enter the word *Virginia* to learn more about this state.

Geography Skills

Five Things to Think About

Geography is the study of Earth. This study sometimes looks at the Earth in five different ways. These ways are the five themes of geography. Each theme is a way of thinking about an area. Look at the examples for this school.

Location

200 Melrose Street

The location of the school is at 200 Melrose Street.

Place

Trees, grass, and other plants grow near the school.

Movement

Some people walk to the school. Others ride to the school in a bus or a car.

Places and People Change Each Other

People put swings and a slide here. Now children can play outside.

Region

This school is in a part of the United States that is near the center of the country.

Regions on Earth

rth is made up of land and water. Some
pictures below show different kinds of
ne picture shows water. Earth has forests,
mountains, and oceans.

The forest has many kinds of trees. Owls, squirrels, and deer live in the forest.

You might see tall grasses growing on the plains. Horses, rabbits, and foxes live here.

Some parts of our country are near the ocean. Many kinds of plants and animals live underwater.

Many parts of our country have very tall mountains. Moose, bears, and big horn sheep live in the mountains.

From Earth to a Globe

Here is a picture that looks down at our Earth. It is a picture taken from space. Earth looks round like a ball.

The smooth blue parts of Earth are water. The other parts with green and brown on them are land. It is very exciting to see Earth this way.

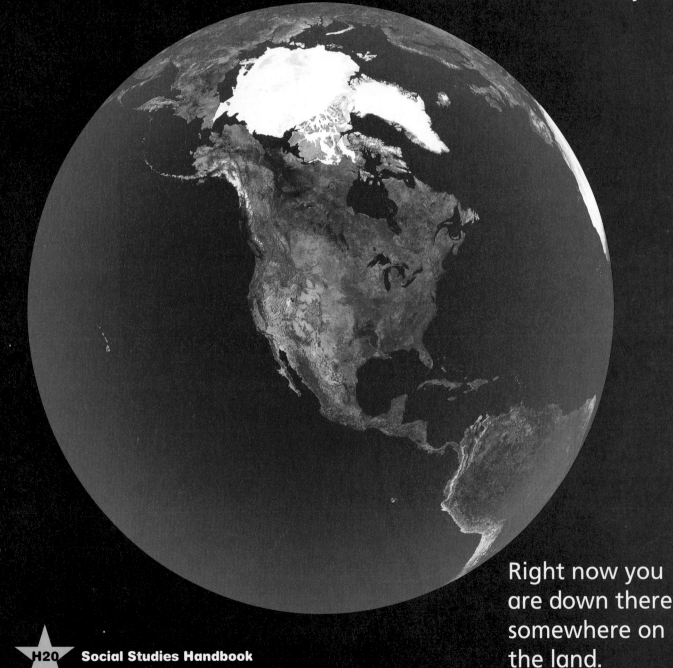

Right now you are down there somewhere on the land.

Vocabulary

globe
Earth
model

The **globe** on this page looks like the picture of **Earth.** A globe is a round **model** of Earth. You can put it on a table. You can turn it and see all around it. You can study it in your class.

You can hold a globe in your hands!

A model is a small copy of something.

Vocabulary

map

From a Picture to a Map

Maybe you do not want to study the whole Earth. Maybe you want to look down only at the area where you live. Your area might look something like this.

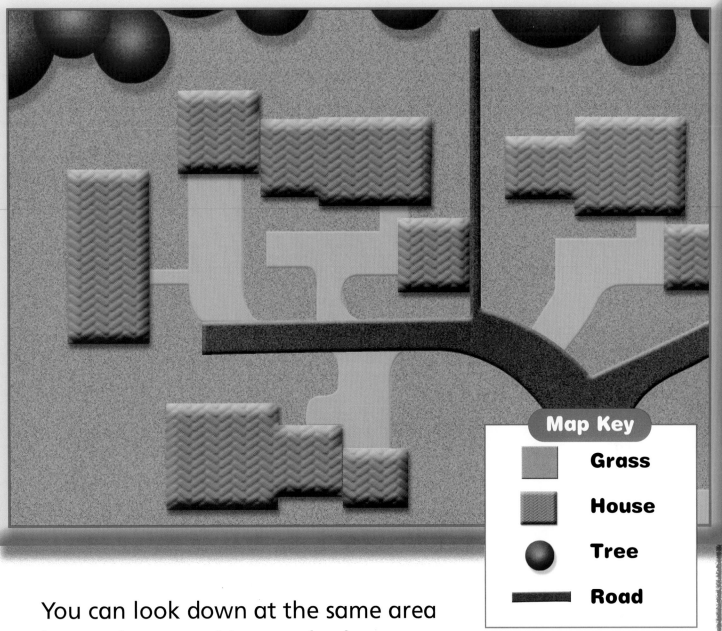

Map Key

Grass

House

Tree

Road

You can look down at the same area in another way. You can look at a map. A **map** is a drawing of a real place as it is seen from above. A map of the same part of town might look like this.

How is the map the same as the picture? How is the map different from the picture?

Look at a Picture of a School

Look at this picture of a school. You can see the walls and the roof of the school.

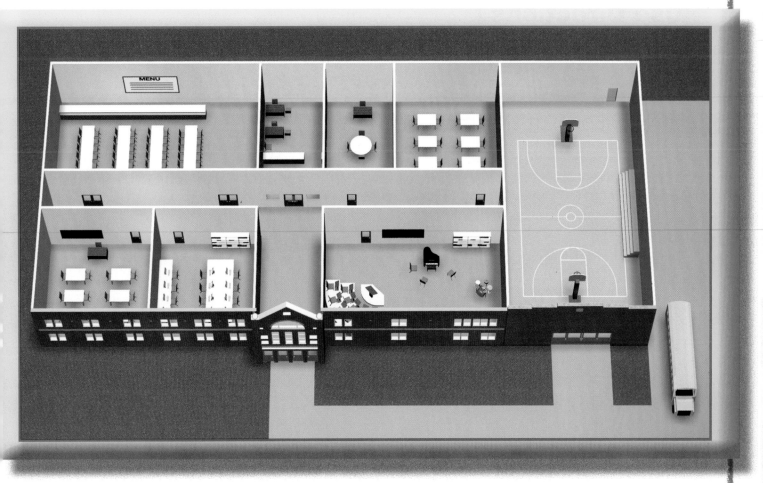

Read a Map of a School

Here is a map that lets you look down inside the same school without the roof. This map shows some of the rooms in the school. Can you point to the cafeteria? What room is the music room next to?

Geography Skills

Use Directions

A map helps you know where things are. Things can be near or far away. They can be between or behind other things. Look at this map of a zoo.

What animal is between the lions and elephants? What animal is farthest away from the monkeys?

Time for School

Why do we go to school?

We Go to School

by Marjorie Sinclair

 Sung to the tune of
"The Farmer in the Dell"

We go to school each day.
We learn in every way.
We learn to read
and write and spell.
We learn to work and play.

3

Vocabulary Preview

school

group

flag

4

country

rule

Andrew at School

Use Picture Clues

Hi. My name is Andrew. I am in first grade. The pictures show some things I do in school. **School** is the place where I learn. Look at the pictures. Then tell about my busy day.

You can learn a lot from pictures. Pictures even help you learn about words. Where do I eat my lunch? What is the name of the place where I go to get a book?

Cafeteria

Library

Try it!

Make a picture book. Draw pictures to show what you do at **school** . Give the book to your partner. Have your partner get clues from your pictures to tell about your day.

Getting to Know Andrew

I have so much to tell you! Look at my pictures. They will help you learn about me. Many of my friends like the same things.

Things I Like

I belong to many groups. A **group** is made up of people or things. People in a group can do things together. Look at the pictures of me in different groups.

My Team

My Family

What did you learn ?

1. Name three things that Andrew likes.

2. Look at the pictures of groups. Tell about each **group.**

3. **Think and Share** Name other groups. Tell who is in each group.

Meet Carl Stotz

1910–1992

Founder of Little League®

Carl Stotz started a baseball league so that groups of children could play baseball together.

Carl played baseball as a boy. The games were not fun. The field was very big. The bats were too heavy. Rules were not followed. Carl wanted to make baseball fun.

Later, Carl Stotz made a baseball field for children. His field looked like a field for adults, but it was smaller. He made the bats smaller and lighter. He made rules for Little League. Today, many children from around the world enjoy playing in Little League!

The first Little League game was played in Williamsport, Pennsylvania.

Carl Stotz with one of the first Little League teams

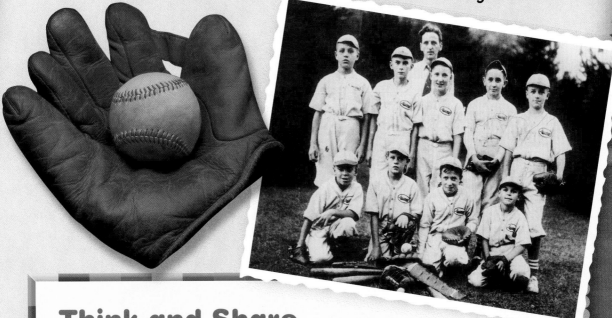

Think and Share

How did Carl Stotz make baseball fun for children to play?

For more information, go online to *Meet the People* at **www.sfsocialstudies.com**.

Families Long Ago

Families from long ago did many things together.

Working

Reading

Eating

Cooking

Playing

Draw a picture of something families do together today.

Home and School

Every morning I eat breakfast. Then I brush my teeth and make my bed. What do you do every morning?

14

My class at school does the same things every morning. We hang up our coats and put our snacks away. Then we sit in our seats.

Every morning, we stand and face the flag. The **flag** stands for our country. A **country** is a land where a group of people live. Our country is the United States of America. We honor our country when we face the flag. Today it is my turn to lead the class. Hooray!

Our Day

Say the Pledge of Allegiance.
Read the calendar.
Work on the computer.
Read a story.
Go outside.

Look at the other things we will do today. We will have a very busy day at school!

What did you learn?

1. What does Andrew do each morning at home? What does he do each morning at school?

2. Why does Andrew's class stand and face the **flag** each day?

3. **Think and Share** Make a list of things that you do each morning. Tell what you do at home. Tell what you do at school.

Ruby went to school in New Orleans, Louisiana.

Ruby Bridges Hall

Ruby was six years old when she began first grade. She was the only African American child in her whole school. African American children had never been allowed to go to that school before. At that time, people were often kept apart because of the color of their skin. Many people in the town did not want Ruby to go to their school. She was very brave. Being brave means having courage.

Ruby as a child

Mrs. Henry and Ruby Bridges Hall

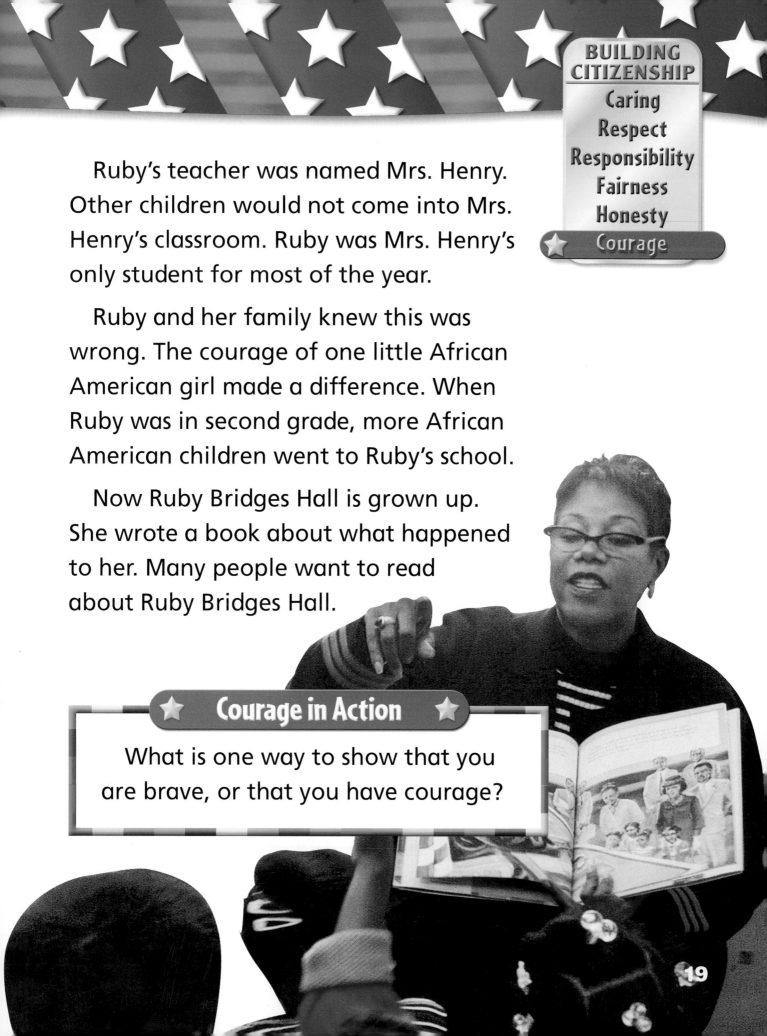

BUILDING CITIZENSHIP

Caring
Respect
Responsibility
Fairness
Honesty
⭐ Courage

Ruby's teacher was named Mrs. Henry. Other children would not come into Mrs. Henry's classroom. Ruby was Mrs. Henry's only student for most of the year.

Ruby and her family knew this was wrong. The courage of one little African American girl made a difference. When Ruby was in second grade, more African American children went to Ruby's school.

Now Ruby Bridges Hall is grown up. She wrote a book about what happened to her. Many people want to read about Ruby Bridges Hall.

⭐ **Courage in Action** ⭐

What is one way to show that you are brave, or that you have courage?

19

Read a Calendar

Every day Andrew's class reads the calendar. A **calendar** is a chart that shows the days, weeks, and months of the year. A calendar helps us remember important days.

September

Sunday	Monday	Tuesday	Wednesday	Thursday	Friday	Saturday
	1 Labor Day	2	3	4	5	6
7	8	9	10	11	12	13
14	15	16	17 Citizenship Day	18	19	20 Mom's Birthday
21	22 First Day of Fall	23	24	25	26	27
28	29	30				

- The name of the month is at the top of the calendar. What month is it?

- Each square is one day. How many days are on this calendar?

- Look at the box that has the number 1 in it. Why is that day important?

Andrew likes the month of February best.
This calendar shows special days in February.

February

Sunday	Monday	Tuesday	Wednesday	Thursday	Friday	Saturday
				1	2 Groundhog Day	3
4	5	6	7	8	9	10
11	12 Lincoln's Birthday	13	14 Valentine's Day	15	16	17
18	19 Presidents' Day	20	21	22 Washington's Birthday	23	24
25 Andrew's Birthday	26	27	28			

What did you learn?

1. What is one reason we use a **calendar**?

2. Why do you think that Andrew likes the month of February the best?

3. **On Your Own** Make a calendar for this month. Label the important days. Why are these days important?

Rules We Follow

We learn many rules in school. A **rule** tells us what to do and what not to do. Our class thought of some rules to follow. Look at the pictures. Tell what rules the children are following.

Raise your hand to talk.

Quiet Please.

Sit quietly.

Do not run in the hallways.

What other rules do you follow at school? What are some rules you follow at home?

Play ball outside.

Pick up your toys.

We have rules at school and at home. Some rules help us work together. Some rules help us stay safe. Look at the pictures. These people help us follow rules at school. Who helps us follow rules at home?

Children must wait until I lead them across the street.

I am a bus driver. Children must sit in their seats when I drive them to school.

I am the principal. I make the rules you follow in school and on the playground.

PRINCIPAL

I am a teacher. My rules help you work together and learn.

I work with the teacher. I help you follow the classroom rules.

What did you learn?

1. Why do we need **rules**?

2. Who helps us follow rules at school?

3. **Think and Share** What might happen if we did not follow rules?

Problem on the Playground

Andrew's class saw a problem. They saw trash on the playground. These are the steps Andrew's class used to solve the problem.

Step 1 Name the problem.

Step 2 Find out more about the problem.

Step 3 List ways to solve the problem.

Step 4 Is one way more useful than another? Talk about the best way to solve the problem.

Step 5 Solve the problem.

Step 6 How well is the problem solved?

Now we have a nice, clean playground!

Try it!

1. What problem did Andrew's class see?

2. What steps did Andrew's class take to solve the problem?

3. **On Your Own** Think of a problem. Tell how you would solve it. Use the steps Andrew's class used.

Learning About My School

Andrew   Our school is so big!

Mr. Jones   Yes, it is. Let me tell you a story about our school.

Mr. Jones Look at these pictures. They give clues about how our school has changed.

Andrew Long ago, our school was in a small building. Why?

Mr. Jones Fewer people lived in this area in the past. We did not have as many children coming to our school then.

Mr. Jones Many people have moved here. Now we have more children. We had to build a bigger school.

Andrew The old school used to be small. Now our school is much bigger. I wonder if my school will get even bigger in the future!

What did you learn?

1. **Use the pictures** to tell how Andrew's school changed.

2. Why did Andrew's school change in size?

3. **Think and Share** Why might your school change in the future? List ways your school might change.

Biography

Meet Mary McLeod Bethune

1875–1955
Educator and Public Speaker

Mary went to a school that had only one room. Later, she started a school for African American girls.

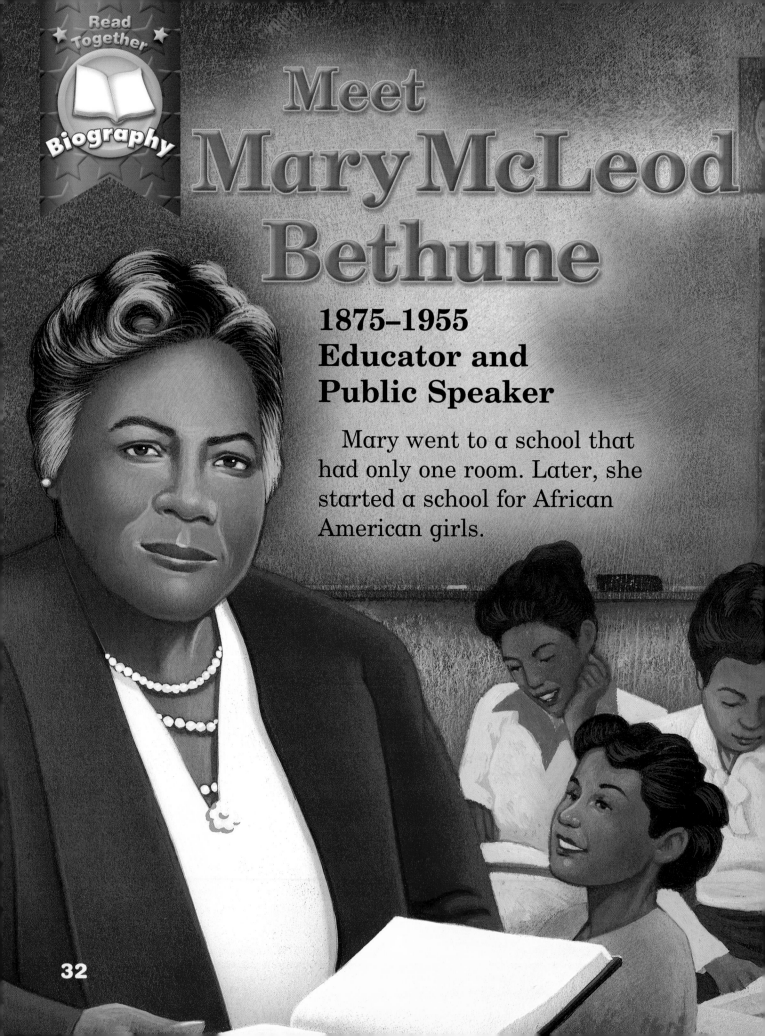

When Mary was a girl, she wanted to learn how to read. Mary could not go to school because there were no schools for African Americans. No one in her family had ever been to school.

When Mary was about nine, she started going to a tiny, one room school. She came home and taught her family what she learned.

When Mary McLeod Bethune became an adult, she started her own school for African American girls. She spoke to groups all around the country. She wanted to help other African Americans. She helped people understand how important it is to have good schools.

Mary McLeod Bethune was born in Mayesville, South Carolina.

Mary McLeod Bethune and a group of students

Think and Share

How did Mary McLeod Bethune help others?

 For more information, go online to *Meet the People* at **www.sfsocialstudies.com**.

Things We Use

These pictures show some things children used at school in the past. What did they use then?

MORE DICK and JANE STORIES

ELSON-GRAY

34

Some things children use at school have changed. Look at the pictures. What do you use today?

Hands-on History

Draw a picture of something you might use in a school of the future. Tell about it.

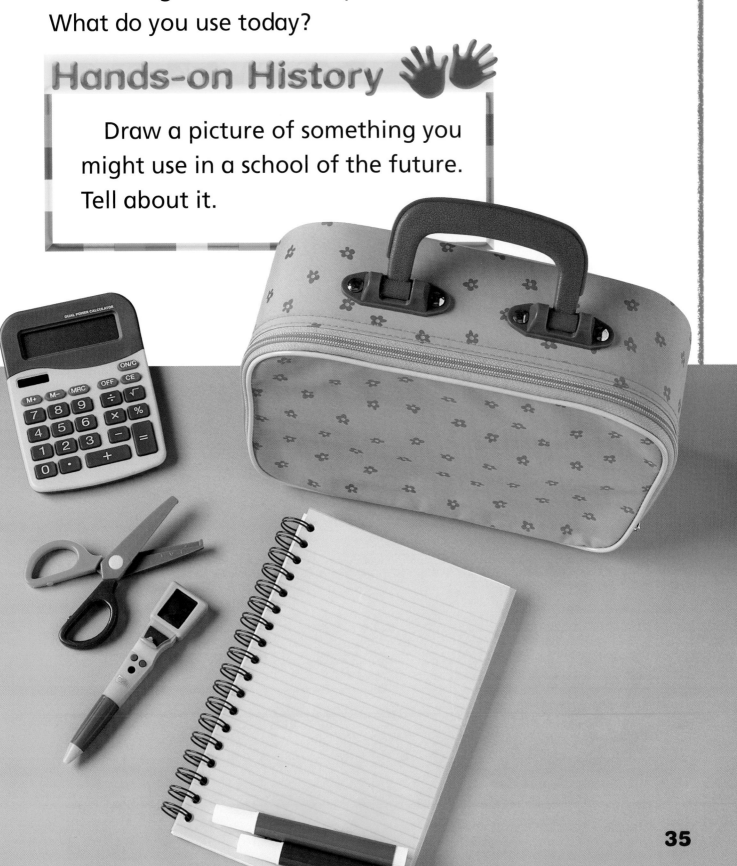

School Today

by Herbert Thomas

What do I do at school?
I sing a song.
I get along.

I learn to read.
I plant a seed.

I read a map.
I sing and clap.

I write and spell.
I show and tell.

I stretch and bend.
I make a friend.
This is what I do at school!

Review

Vocabulary Review

flag
school
rule
country

Match each word to its picture.

1.

2.

3.

4.

★ ★ ★ ★ ★ ★ ★ ★

 Which word completes each sentence?

1. When you play on a team, you are part of a _____.

   a. rule   **b.** map

   c. group   **d.** country

2. We learn to work together and stay safe when we follow a _____.

   a. rule   **b.** flag

   c. map   **d.** country

Skills Review

Use Picture Clues

Look at these pictures.
Tell what is happening.

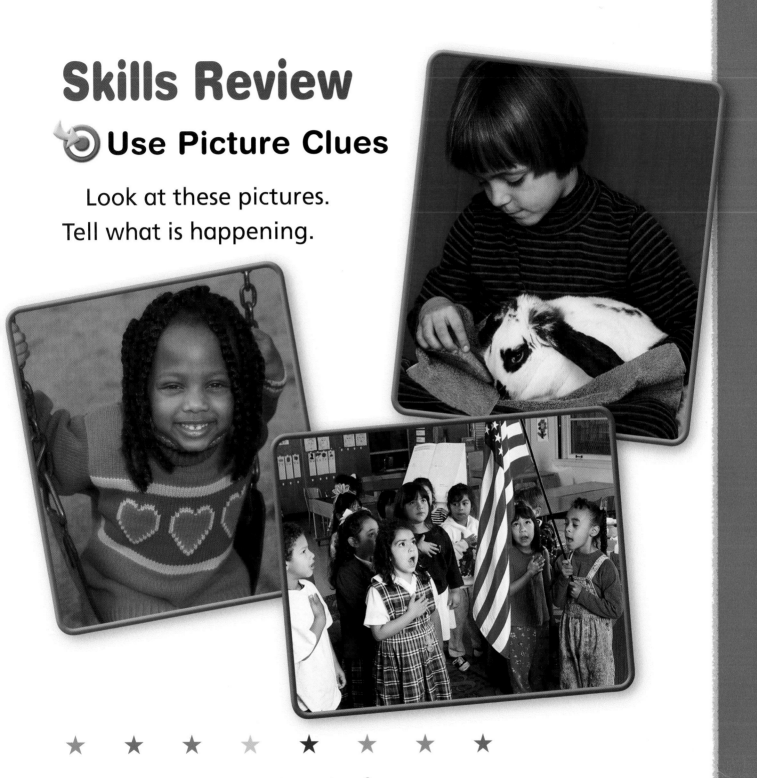

★ ★ ★ ★ ★ ★ ★ ★

Problem Solving

Your cafeteria is too noisy. Tell steps
you would take to solve the problem.

Skills Review

Read a Calendar

1. How many days are in this month?

2. When is Veterans Day?

3. What day of the week is November 16?

November						
Sunday	**Monday**	**Tuesday**	**Wednesday**	**Thursday**	**Friday**	**Saturday**
		1	2	3	4	5
6	7	8 VOTE! Election Day	9	10	11 Veterans Day	12
13	14	15	16	17	18	19
20	21	22	23	24 Thanksgiving Day	25	26
27	28	29	30			

Skills On Your Own

Draw a calendar of your favorite month. Mark the important days.

What did you learn?

1. Name two different groups.

2. What are two rules that help you work together? What are two rules that keep you safe?

3. Why is it important to follow rules?

4. **Think and Share** Think of rules for your class. Make a list of your rules. Share your rules with the class.

Test Talk

Look for key words in the question.

Read About School

Look for books like these in the library.

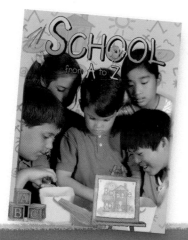

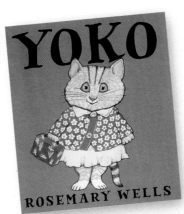

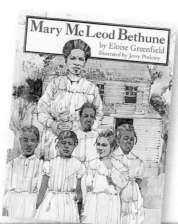

UNIT 1 Project

Follow Me!

Give a video tour of your school.

1 Think about what some important places are in your school. What happens in each place?

2 Draw a picture that shows what happens in one of the important places.

3 Make a model of a video camera.

4 Use your model camera to give a video tour. Describe the place you drew in your picture. Tell what visitors would need to know about your important place.

Internet Activity

Go to www.sfsocialstudies.com/activities to learn more about schools.

In My Community

What do you like best about where you live? Why?

This Is My Community

by Carlos Elliot

 Sung to the tune of "Twinkle, Twinkle, Little Star"

This is where I live and play,
Work and shop most every day.

Here's my home and here's my street.
This is where my neighbors meet.

Lots of people live near me.
This is my community!

45

neighborhood

community

law

leader

state

continent

ocean

Where Kim Lives

Alike and Different

Hello! I'm Kim. This is my home.

Homes can come in many shapes and sizes. They can be made of wood, brick, or stone. Homes can be for one person or for many people.

Homes can look alike. **Alike** means how things are the same. Homes can also look different from each other. **Different** means how things are not the same. Look at these pictures. How are the homes alike? How are they different?

Try it!

Draw pictures of two homes. Tell how they are **alike** and **different.**

Welcome to My Neighborhood

My home has an address. An address can help you find a home or another building. An address has a number and a street name. My address is 9 Maple Street.

Maple Street

Look on the map. Find my home. Now find my school. What is the address of my school?

Pine Street

Blue Street

Maple Street

My home and school are part of my neighborhood. A **neighborhood** is a place where people live, work, and play.

Neighborhoods can be big or small. They can be noisy or quiet. They can have many buildings or just a few buildings.

Tell how these neighborhoods are alike and different.

Meet some people who work in my neighborhood.

I pick up the trash.

My mom works in a shop.

I deliver the mail

What did you learn?

1. What is a **neighborhood?**

2. Name three kinds of work people can do in a neighborhood.

3. **Think and Share** Write about your neighborhood. Tell how it is **alike** and **different** from the neighborhoods shown in the pictures.

Use a Map Key

Some maps use pictures to stand for real things. A picture that stands for a real thing is called a **symbol.** On this map, the 🌳 stands for a tree.

Rose Street

This is a map of the park near Kim's home. The map has a map key. A **map key** tells what the symbols on the map mean.

Map Key

trash can

swing set

drinking fountain

park bench

tree

street

Try it!

1. Why are **symbols** on a map important?

2. What is next to the in the park?

3. **On Your Own** Draw a map and **map key** of your classroom. Show how you go from your desk to your teacher's desk.

Different Kinds of Communities

I live in a big city.

My neighborhood is part of a community. A **community** is a group of people and the place where they live. A community is bigger than a neighborhood. Many different neighborhoods can be part of a community.

A city is a big community. Many people live and work in the city.

Some people live in a town. A town community is not as big as a city.

Some people live in a suburb. A suburb is a community near a big city.

The homes in a farm community can be far away from each other.

What did you learn

1. What is a **community?**

2. How is a city community different from a town community?

3. **Think and Share** Tell how your community is alike and different from these communities.

How a Community Changed

This picture shows what Kim's community looked like in the past. Her community has changed since then.

This is Kim's community today. More people live and work in her community now. The community has more homes and stores. Look how it has changed.

Hands-on History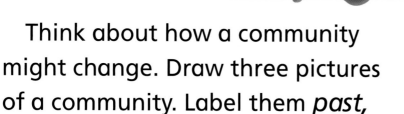

Think about how a community might change. Draw three pictures of a community. Label them *past, today,* and *future.*

Use Four Directions

Kim uses the directions on a map to find places in her community. **Directions** tell her which way to go. North, south, east, and west are the four main directions.

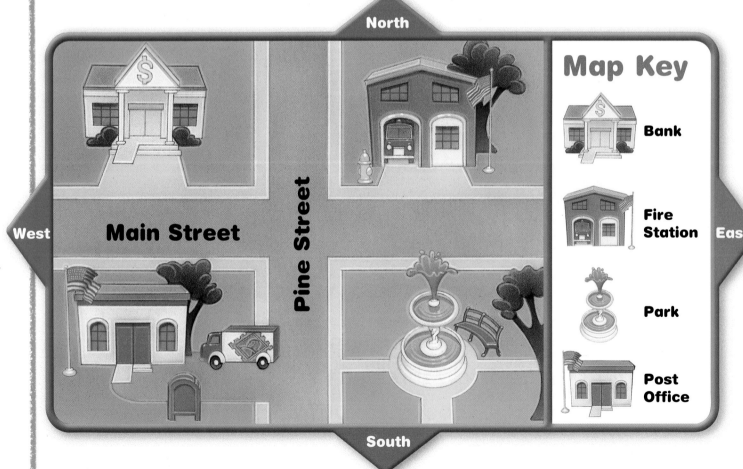

North

West

Main Street

Pine Street

East

South

Map Key

Bank

Fire Station

Park

Post Office

Put your finger on Pine Street. Move your finger toward the arrow that points south. You are moving south. Now move your finger toward the arrow that points north. Which direction are you moving? When you face north, east is on your right. What direction is on your left?

Try it!

1. Is the park north or south of Main Street?

2. Find the fire station. What **direction** would you go to get to the bank?

3. **On Your Own** Stand by your desk. Face north. Tell where things are in your classroom and school. Use the words *north, south, east,* and *west.*

Special Things We Do

People in my community share different customs. A custom is the way people usually do something. My scrapbook has pictures of special customs we have.

We have a picnic on Independence Day. It is our country's birthday.

We give a basket of fruit to new neighbors. Welcome to our neighborhood!

I make my mother a special gift every Mother's Day.

Our friends go to a parade
every year on Chinese New Year.
Last year we went with them.

My mom and I read a book each night before bedtime. This is our special time together!

What did you learn ?

1. What special times does your family share?

2. Why do we celebrate Independence Day?

3. **Think and Share** Draw a picture of one way to celebrate a special day. Tell what is happening in your picture.

Chinese New Year

Man Po is nine years old and lives in China. She likes Chinese New Year. It is one of the world's most colorful celebrations.

Thousands of people watch the floats in the New Year parade.

Tangerines with leaves are often called the lucky fruits of the New Year.

This float is sometimes in the New Year parade.

Some Chinese believe that peach blossoms are lucky.

Some people think a kumquat tree brings good luck.

"My outfit is made of silk. It is very beautiful."

恭喜發財

"I have written words in Chinese that wish a person riches."

On New Years morning, Chinese children get money in red envelopes.

One of Man Po's favorite foods is Law Pak Ko, a cake with shrimps.

Law Pak Ko

Red is the main color for clothes and decorations at New Year. It is a color of happiness.

67

Harriet Tubman

Harriet Tubman was born in Dorchester County, Maryland.

Some customs and ways of life have changed from long ago. Harriet Tubman lived in our country when some African Americans were not free. She wanted fair treatment for everyone.

Harriet Tubman worked hard so people could be treated fairly. She helped many African Americans move to new places where they could be free. The people she helped followed a special path in the woods. The path was called the Underground Railroad.

Harriet Tubman

BUILDING CITIZENSHIP
Caring
Respect
Responsibility
Fairness
Honesty
Courage

Harriet Tubman was a very brave woman. Today we remember her as a leader who believed in fairness and freedom for African Americans.

House on the Underground Railroad

★ **Fairness in Action** ★

What can you and your classmates do to be sure everyone is treated fairly?

Community Laws and Leaders

I am Officer Taylor. I make sure you follow laws.

A **law** is a rule that people must obey. Laws help keep us safe. They also help keep communities clean.

Look at these signs. They show different laws. Kim has all these signs in her community. Which laws keep people safe? Which law keeps the community clean?

NO SWIMMING

STOP

70

A mayor is a leader of a community. A **leader** helps people decide what to do.

Mayor Garza works with other community leaders. They make decisions about their community. They make their community a great place to live!

I am Mayor Garza. I am mayor of a small town.

What did you learn?

1. Why do we need rules and **laws**?

2. What do **leaders** do? Who are the leaders in your school and community?

3. **Think and Share** Think of two laws. Draw signs for them. Share your signs.

71

Meet Jane Addams

1860–1935
Social Worker

Jane Addams was a famous community leader. She started a special place for people in her community.

When she was growing up, Jane learned how important it was to help others. As an adult, Jane Addams and a friend took over a big, empty house in Chicago, Illinois. They called it Hull House.

Hull House became a place where people in the community could go to get help. Some people went to Hull House because they were sick. Others went because they had questions about the law. Some people needed care for their children. People also went there to take classes. Hull House had a community kitchen, playground, and nursery.

In 1931, Jane Addams was the first American woman to win an important prize called the Nobel Peace Prize.

Jane Addams was born in Cedarville, Illinois.

Hull House Museum

Think and Share

How did Jane Addams help people in the community?

For more information, go online to *Meet the People* at **www.sfsocialstudies.com.**

5

Where in the World Do I Live?

Here is my community. My community is a city called Miami. I live in the state of Florida. A **state** is part of a country.

The United States of America is my country. We have fifty states in the United States. What is the name of your state? Find it on the map.

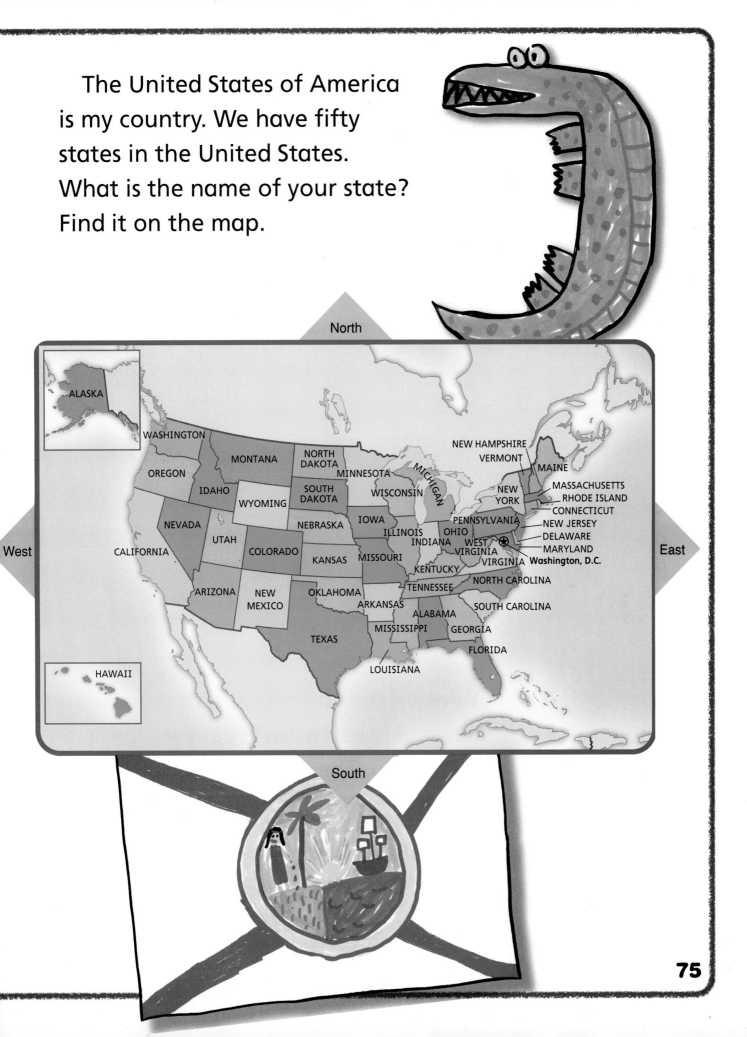

North

West

East

South

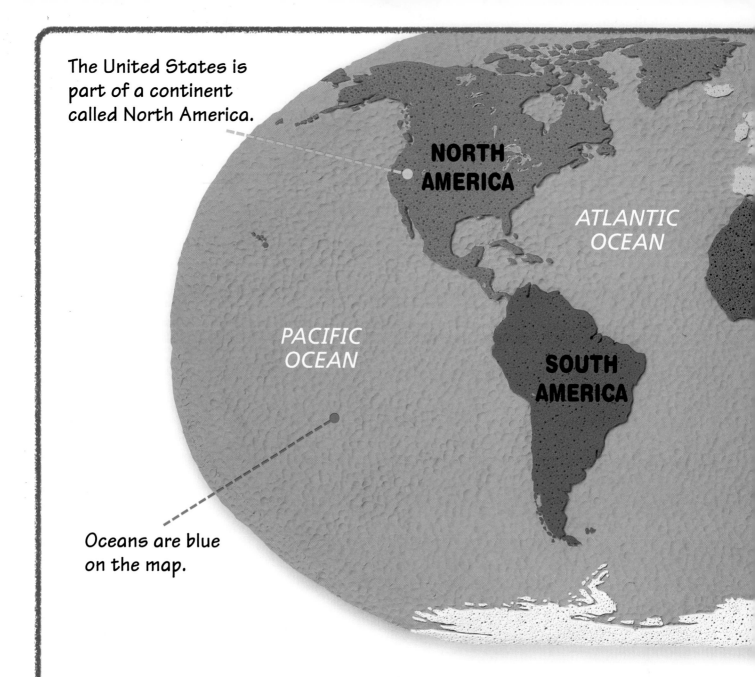

The United States is part of a continent called North America.

NORTH AMERICA

ATLANTIC OCEAN

PACIFIC OCEAN

SOUTH AMERICA

Oceans are blue on the map.

I live on the continent of North America. A **continent** is a very large piece of land. The world has seven continents. Find them on the map.

The world has four oceans too. An **ocean** is a very large body of water. Ocean water is very salty.

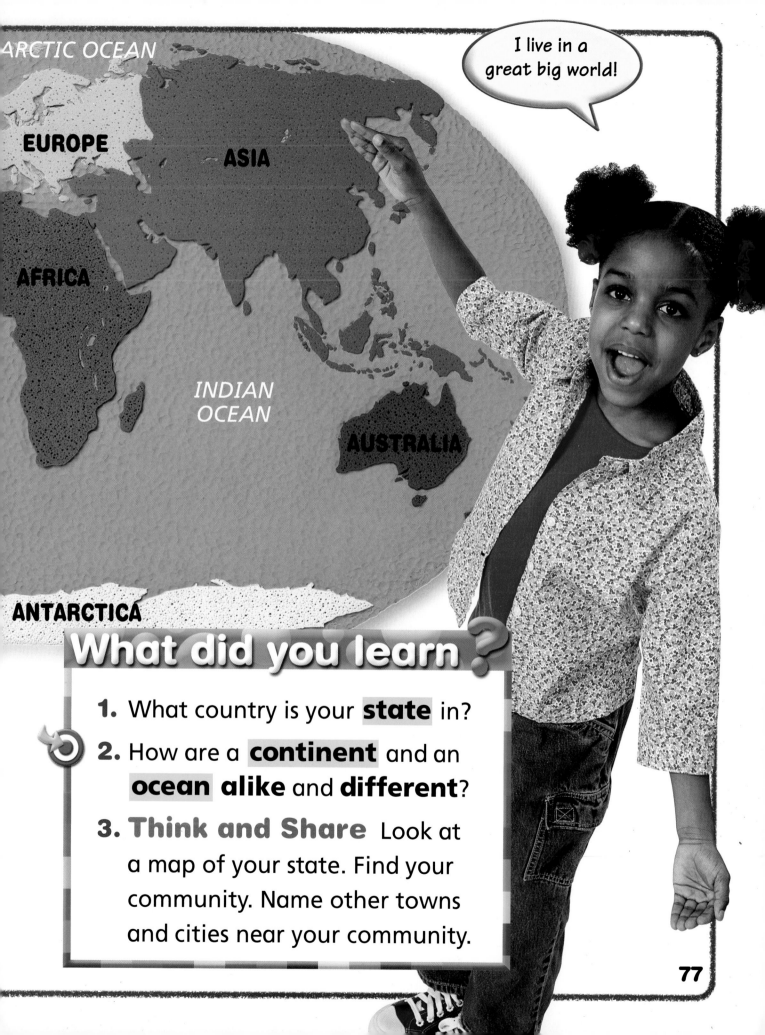

I live in a great big world!

EUROPE

ASIA

AFRICA

INDIAN OCEAN

AUSTRALIA

ANTARCTICA

What did you learn?

1. What country is your **state** in?

2. How are a **continent** and an **ocean alike** and **different**?

3. **Think and Share** Look at a map of your state. Find your community. Name other towns and cities near your community.

77

Meet Henry Flagler

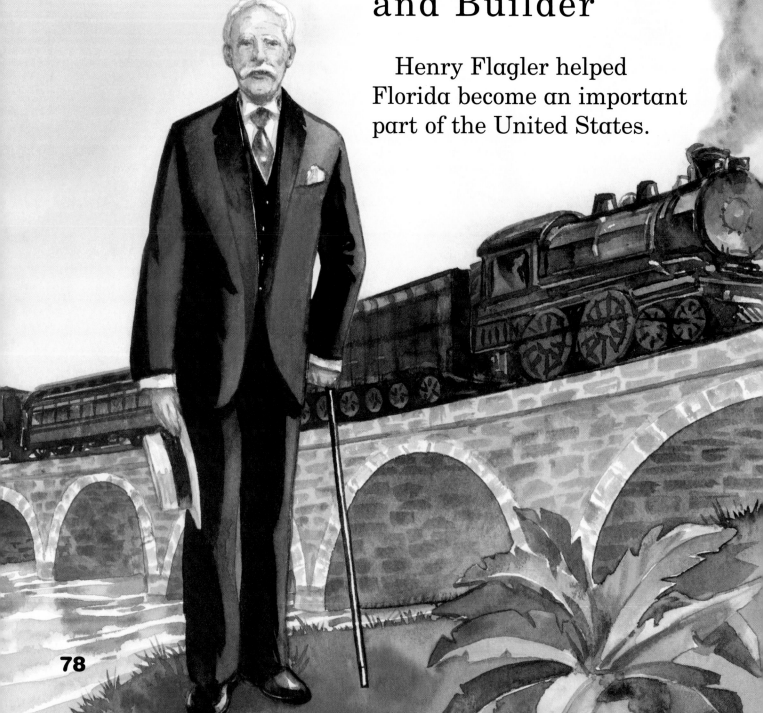

1830–1913
Businessman
and Builder

Henry Flagler helped
Florida become an important
part of the United States.

Young Henry got his first job when he was fourteen years old. He worked very hard. Soon, Henry Flagler and other businessmen started the Standard Oil Company.

Henry Flagler was born in Hopewell, New York.

Henry Flagler moved to Florida. At that time if people came to visit Florida, there were not many places to stay. Before long, Henry Flagler built a hotel in St. Augustine.

Later, Henry Flagler bought a railroad. His railroad soon went to many cities throughout Florida. Henry Flagler built many big, beautiful hotels in these cities.

Ponce de Leon Hotel

Henry Flagler's railroad and hotels made it possible for many people to visit Florida. This helped the state to grow and become an important part of the United States.

Think and Share

What are two ways Henry Flagler helped Florida?

For more information, go online to *Meet the People* at **www.sfsocialstudies.com**.

One Great Big Community
by Toni Barkley

Here is my home.
It's very tall.
It's just the right size
To fit us all.

Here is my neighborhood
All around me.
It's part of a bigger
Community.

Here is my state.
It's one of fifty.
It's part of my country.
It's very nifty!

Here is my world.
It's special, you see.
It's the perfect home
For you and me!

81

Vocabulary Review

Tell which word completes each sentence.

neighborhood

continent

ocean

leader

state

1. People live, work, and play in a _____.

2. A mayor is a community _____.

3. Florida is a _____.

4. A very large piece of land is a _____.

5. A very large body of salt water is called an _____.

★ ★ ★ ★ ★ ★ ★ ★

 TEST PREP

Which word completes the sentence?

1. A rule you must obey is a _____.

   a. law   **b.** state

   c. leader   **d.** community

2. A city is a big _____.

   a. neighborhood   **b.** continent

   c. ocean   **d.** community

Skills Review

Alike and Different

Tell or write about how laws can be **alike** and **different**.

Use a Map Key

1. What does 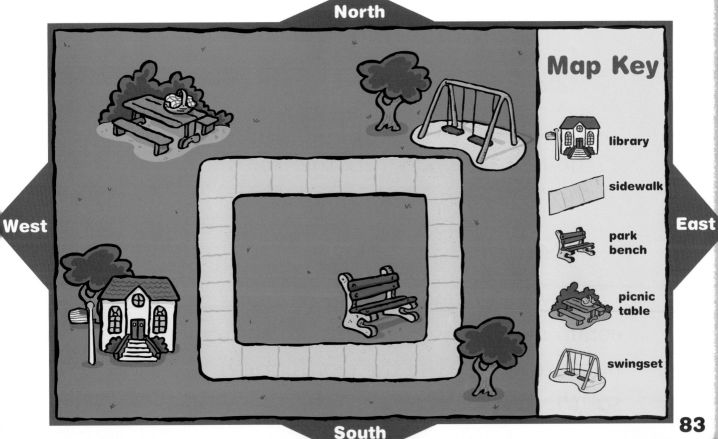 stand for?

2. How many symbols are on the map key?

3. Draw a symbol for something on the map that is not in the map key.

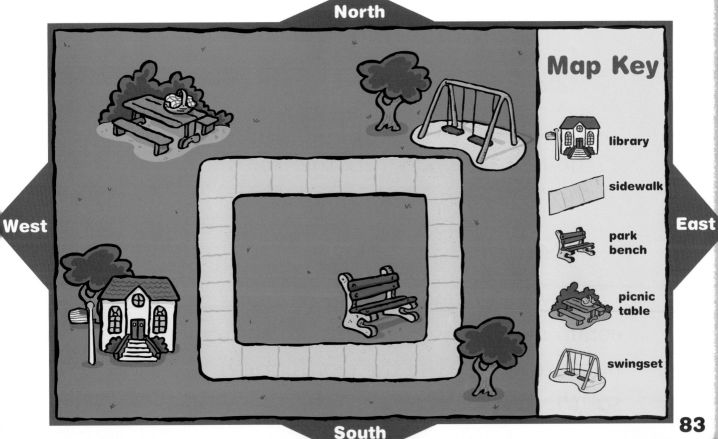

North

West

East

South

Map Key

library

sidewalk

park bench

picnic table

swingset

Skills Review
Use Four Directions

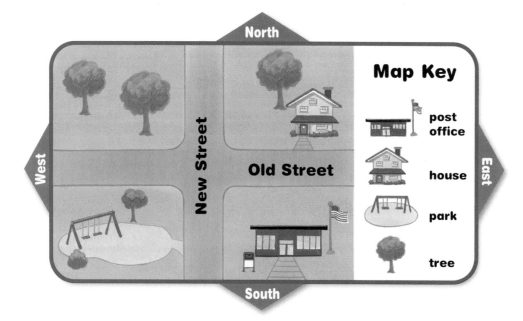

1. Is the house north or south of Old Street?

2. What place is west of New Street?

3. Tell how you would go from the house to the park. Use the words *north, south, east,* or *west.*

Skills On Your Own

Draw a map and map key of your community. Tell how you would go from home to school. Use the words *north, south, east,* and *west.*

What did you learn?

1. Why is it important to know your home address?

2. How can you live in a community and state at the same time?

Test Talk

Find key words in the text.

3. Name two ways a community might change over time.

4. **Write and Share** Write about a mayor and a principal. Tell how these leaders are **alike** and **different.**

Read About Communities

Look for books like these in the library.

Where I Live
Christopher Wormell

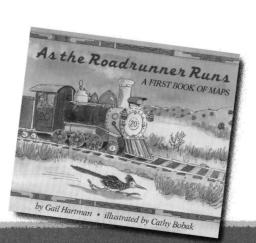

As the Roadrunner Runs
A FIRST BOOK OF MAPS

by Gail Hartman • illustrated by Cathy Bobak

LONG AGO and TODAY
A Home Album
Peter and Connie Roop

2 Project

News for All

TV news reporters tell us what goes on in the world. You can report what goes on in your community.

1 Choose an event that happened or might happen in your community.

2 Make a poster about the event. At the bottom of your poster, write words that describe what is happening.

3 Give a news report about the event. Tell what happened and who was there. Tell when and where the event happened. Tell why it is news.

Internet Activity

Go to www.sfsocialstudies.com/activities to learn more about communities.

Work! Work! Work!

What kinds of work would you like to do?

Lots of Jobs

by Latrice Butler

 Sung to the tune of
"Skip to My Lou"

Baker, teacher,
doctor, too.

Lots of jobs
I'd like to do.

Care for animals
in the zoo.

What kinds of work
would you do?

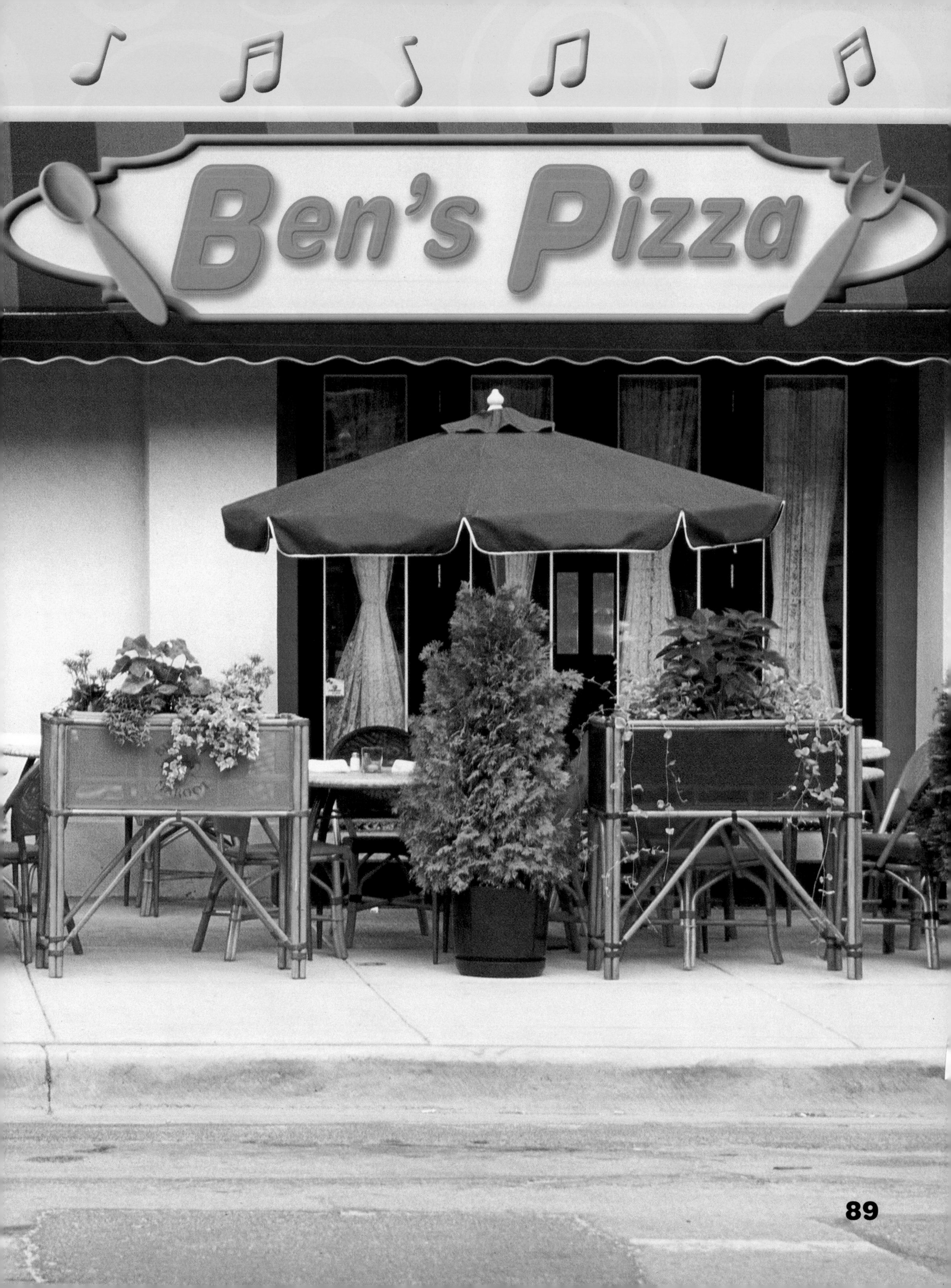
Ben's Pizza

Vocabulary Preview

job

needs

wants

tools

goods

service

volunteer

transportation

UNIT 3

Ben at Work

Target Skill

Put Things in Order

Hi! I'm Ben. Someday I want to own a pizza shop.

Saturday I had a lemonade stand. These pictures show the order in which things happened. Use your own words to tell what I did.

First

Next

Did you use words like **first, next,** and **last?** Those words tell the order in which things happened.

First, I made the lemonade.

Next, I set up my stand.

Last, I sold a cup to my friend.

Look for **first, next,** and **last** as you learn more about people at work.

Last

Try it!

Tell or write about how Ben could make a pizza. Use the words **first, next,** and **last.** Draw pictures to show the order in which things happen.

Ben's Jobs

I do lots of jobs to help at home. A **job** is the work people do. **First,** I put away my toys all by myself.

Next, I feed our dog. My whole family takes turns caring for Rusty.

Last, my family and I work together
to make dinner. I like to help cook.
When the work is done, we all eat.
I like that part the best!

I have jobs at school. My big job is to learn. That is your job at school too.

Today I have a special job. I get to feed our hamster. What are your special jobs at school?

What did you learn?

1. What is a **job**? Why are jobs in your classroom important?

2. How are jobs at home and at school the same? How are they different?

3. **Think and Share** Tell or write about a job you do well. Use the words **first, next,** and **last** in your story.

Use a Chart

A **chart** is a way to show things using words and pictures. This chart shows some special jobs children do in school.

Jobs at School

Jobs	Helpers
Feed hamster.	Ben
Water plants.	Mary
Clean board.	Sam

- The title tells what the chart is about. What is this chart about?

- The left side of the chart lists the jobs.

- Look at the name next to the first job. Which helper feeds the hamster?

Ben and his sister Rita have jobs at home. This chart shows the jobs they do. Use the chart to answer the questions.

Jobs at Home

Jobs	Helper
Set table.	Ben
Clear table.	Rita
Walk dog.	Ben
Feed dog.	Rita

1. Who clears the table?

2. Who walks the dog?

3. On Your Own Make a **chart** to show the jobs your family does at home.

Needs and Wants

My family gives me many things I need. **Needs** are the things we must have to live. The pictures show some needs people have.

We need food and water to help us stay well and grow.

We need clothes to keep us warm.

We need a place to live.

100

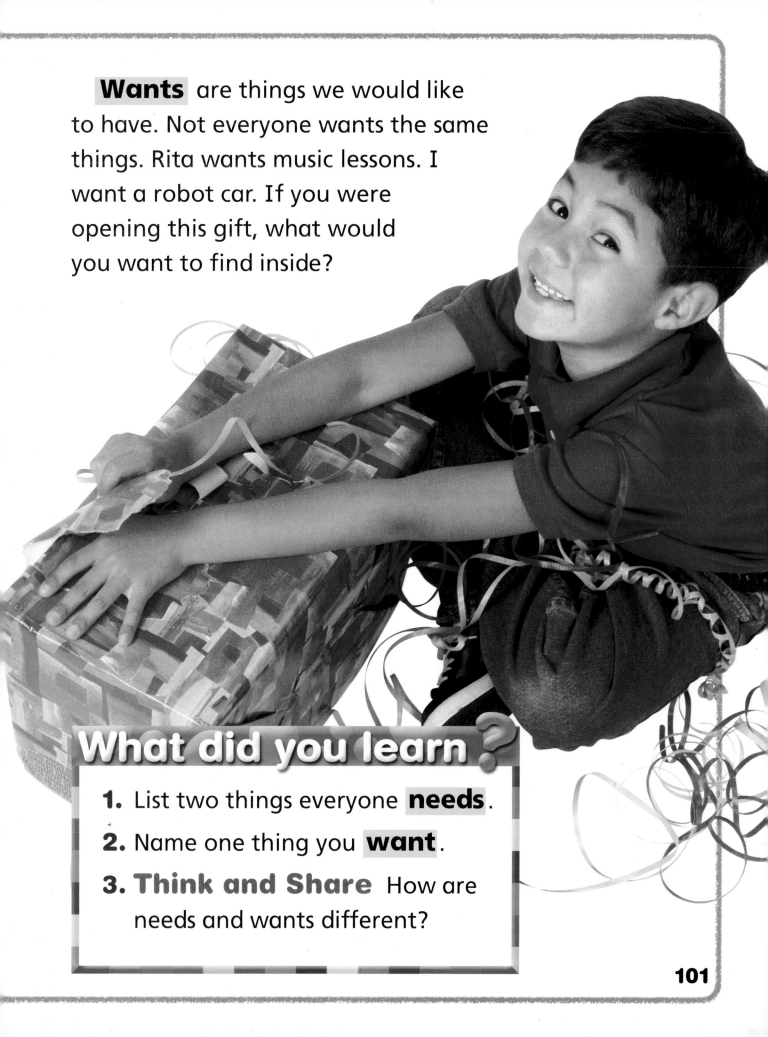

Wants are things we would like to have. Not everyone wants the same things. Rita wants music lessons. I want a robot car. If you were opening this gift, what would you want to find inside?

What did you learn?

1. List two things everyone **needs**.

2. Name one thing you **want**.

3. **Think and Share** How are needs and wants different?

Changing Toys

Ben wants a robot car. Children have always played with toys. These are toys that children have wanted then and now.

Then	Now

Where on the chart would you put these toys?

Hands-on History

Think about a new toy children might want in the future. Draw a picture of it.

3

Spending and Saving

I earned 70¢ from my lemonade stand. Now I can choose how to spend it. Here are some things I want to buy. Some of these cost more money than I have. What would you do?

75¢

25¢

90¢

85¢

50¢

I can spend my money now or save it for later. To save money means to put it away to use at another time. After my next lemonade stand, I'll have even more money!

What did you learn?

1. Name two things people can do with their money.

2. What can families choose to do if they want something that costs more money than they have?

3. **Think and Share** Why do people save money?

Money Around the World

People all over the world spend and save money.

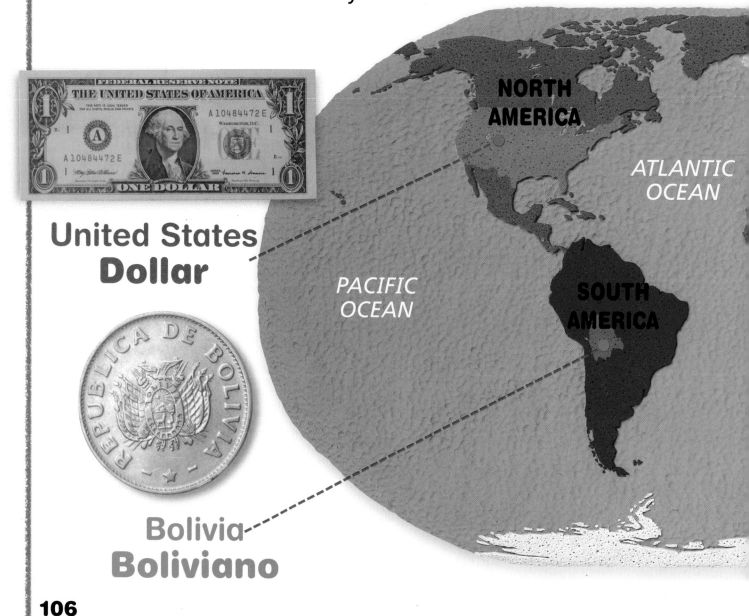

United States Dollar

Bolivia Boliviano

NORTH AMERICA

ATLANTIC OCEAN

PACIFIC OCEAN

SOUTH AMERICA

Poland
Zloty

Japan
Yen

ARCTIC OCEAN

EUROPE

ASIA

AFRICA

INDIAN
OCEAN

AUSTRALIA

Central Bank of Egypt

ONE POUND

ANTARCTICA

Australia
Dollar

Egypt
Pound

Welcome to Job Day!

Workers have come to our class to tell us about the work they do. Some workers use tools. **Tools** are things that are used to help people do work. Some workers earn money by growing or making goods. Things that are grown or made are **goods.**

I make computers.

My dad is a peanut farmer.

Samira

Some workers earn money by having service jobs. A **service** is a job people do to help others. It helps people meet their wants and needs. Do you know someone who has a service job? What does the person do?

My dad is a plumber. He fixes broken pipes.

I help children learn. I am a teacher.

Some people do not earn money for their work. They are volunteers. A **volunteer** works for free. Volunteers help others.

We help people who need food, clothing, or a place to stay.

Food Drive

There are many kinds of jobs. Which would you choose? All kinds of work are important! How do all these workers help us?

What did you learn?

1. What are some **services** that help us?

2. How do **volunteers** help people?

3. **Think and Share** Name three **goods** you use every day. How do you use them?

Kid's Kitchen is in Warner Robins, Georgia.

Kid's Kitchen

When Sagen was in second grade, she saw something interesting on TV. It was about helping her community. She decided to be a volunteer.

Sagen started a group called Kid's Kitchen. The group gives lunch to families in need. It is open one day a week.

Sagen

BUILDING CITIZENSHIP

⭐ **Caring**

Respect
Responsibility
Fairness
Honesty
Courage

Many children volunteer. They make hundreds of sandwiches each week. Some people take home leftovers for dinner.

"When I tell someone about Kid's Kitchen, I hope it will inspire them to do something in their town," says Sagen.

⭐ **Caring in Action** ⭐

What can you do to show you care for someone?

113

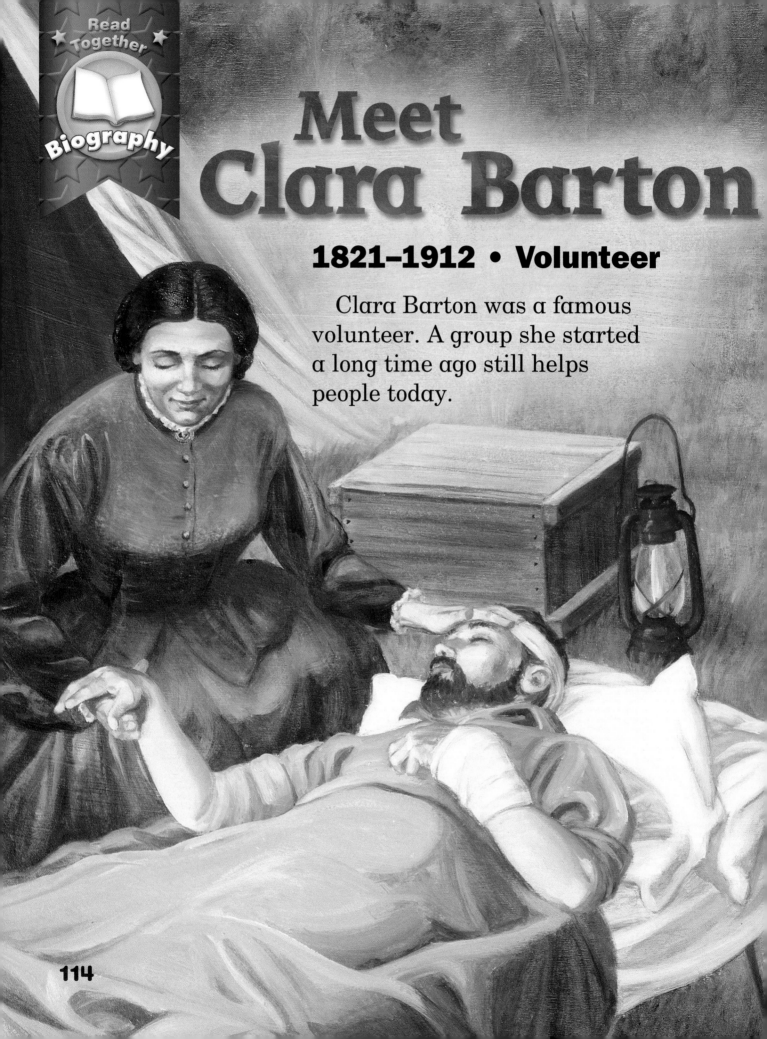

Meet Clara Barton

1821–1912 • Volunteer

Clara Barton was a famous volunteer. A group she started a long time ago still helps people today.

Clara Barton worked hard to help people. When she was just a girl, she helped take care of her brother. He was sick for about two years!

During the Civil War, Clara Barton was a volunteer. She helped soldiers who were hurt. She handed out bandages and medicine. Her work saved many lives.

After the war, Clara Barton wanted to keep on helping people. She started the American Red Cross. Today the Red Cross gives food, clothing, and shelter to people who need help all over the world.

Clara Barton was born in Oxford, Massachusetts.

American Red Cross

Clara Barton made a red cross from a ribbon she wore.

Think and Share

Tell two ways Clara Barton helped people.

For more information, go online to *Meet the People* at **www.sfsocialstudies.com.**

Interview with a Farmer

Mr. Ford   I grow peanuts.

Ben   I love peanuts! How do you grow them?

Mr. Ford   It takes a lot of work to grow peanuts.

First, I plant the peanuts. They start to grow.

Next, I take care of them as they grow.

Last, I pull them up.

Ben How do peanuts get from the farm to me?

Mr. Ford

First, a truck takes the peanuts to the factory.

Next, they are dried, cleaned, and roasted.

Last, they are put into bags and sent to the stores.

Ben The peanuts go from the farm to me with a lot of help from people who work!

What did you learn?

1. Tell about some of the work a farmer does.

2. Tell how peanuts get from the farm to the store. Use the words **first, next,** and **last.**

3. **Think and Share** What are some goods from a farm that you use every day?

119

Follow a Route

The map shows the route the truck takes from the farm to the factory. A **route** is one way to get from one place to another.

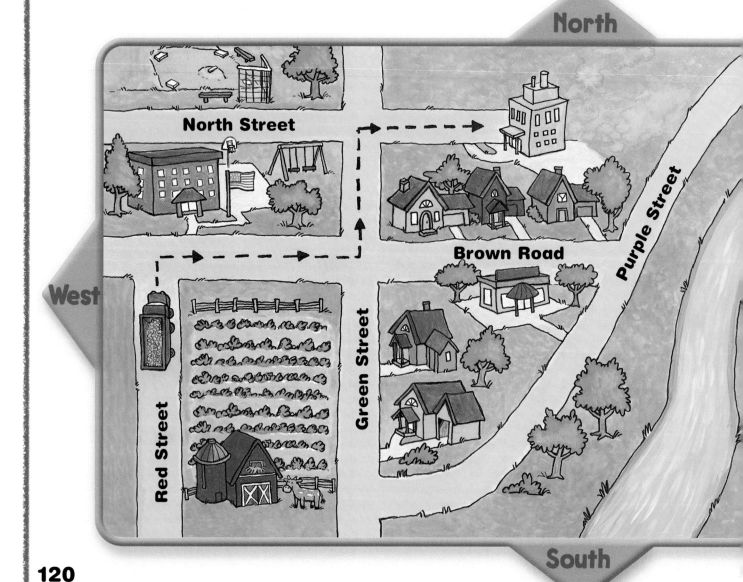

Look at the map. Tell what building is just north of the truck. What does the arrow show? Where does the route begin? Follow the route with your finger.

Map Key

 Farm

 Store

 Factory

 School

 House

 Truck Route

East

Try it!

1. What does the stand for? How do you know?

2. What direction does the truck go on each street?

3. **On Your Own** Make a map and a map key of your school. Tell what **route** you would take to get from your classroom to the office.

Meet George Washington Carver

About 1864–1943

Scientist and Teacher

George Washington Carver's job was to help farmers. He showed them how to plant and use peanuts.

As a young boy, George liked plants. Later, he went to school to learn about plants and farming. He became a teacher to help farmers.

George Washington Carver taught farmers how to grow peanuts. He knew that peanut plants help to make the soil healthy so other crops can grow. He also made many new things from peanuts. You may even use some of the things he learned to make. Did you know that soap, candy, and paint can be made from peanuts?

George Washington Carver was born in Diamond Grove, Missouri.

Peanuts with roots and stems

Think and Share

How did George Washington Carver's work help people?

For more information, go online to *Meet the People* at **www.sfsocialstudies.com.**

Lesson 6

From Place to Place

Mr. Ford drives a tractor and a truck on his farm. The tractor and truck are his transportation. **Transportation** moves people and goods from place to place.

Sometimes Ben travels by bike or car. What kinds of transportation do you use?

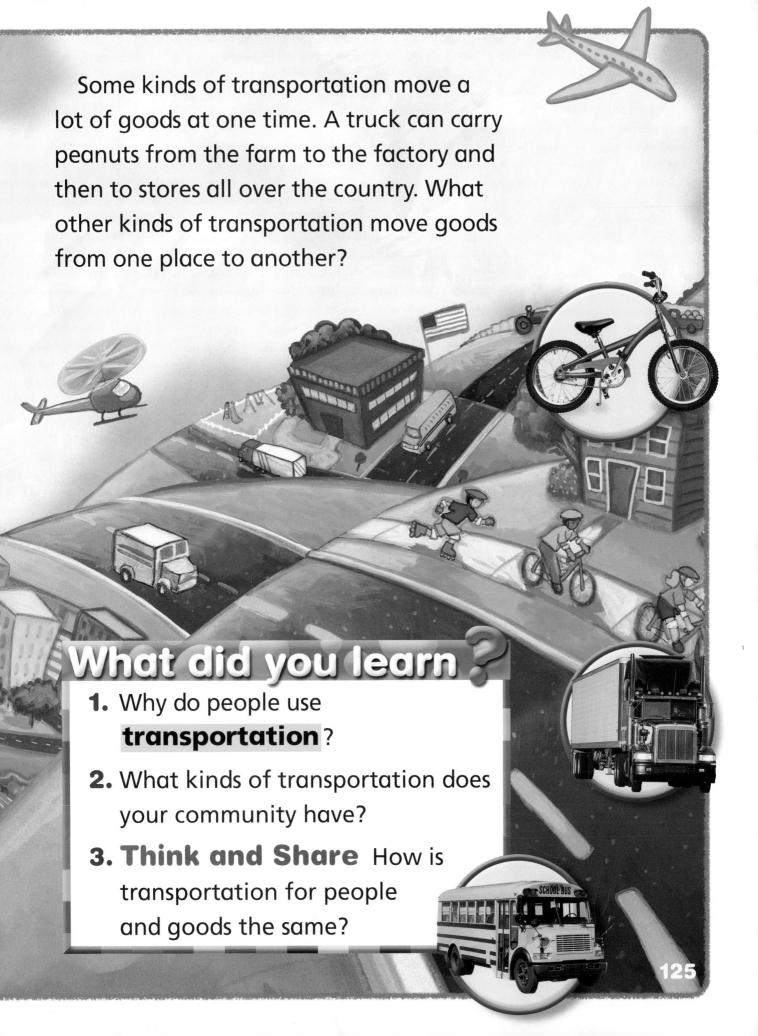

Some kinds of transportation move a lot of goods at one time. A truck can carry peanuts from the farm to the factory and then to stores all over the country. What other kinds of transportation move goods from one place to another?

What did you learn

1. Why do people use **transportation**?

2. What kinds of transportation does your community have?

3. **Think and Share** How is transportation for people and goods the same?

Big Wheels

Look at some types of transportation.
What jobs do these trucks help people do?

concrete truck

mixing drum

hood

tank

wheels

126

cab

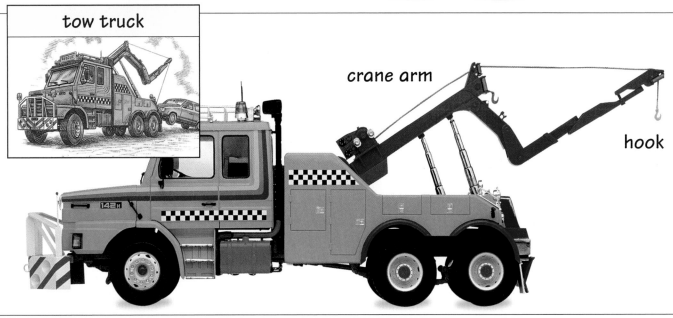

crane arm

hook

bumper

127

End with a Poem

Work Day
by Kate Greenwood

My mom and I
went to work today.

Well, she went to work
and I went to play.

She met with people
and talked on the phone.

I wonder what I'll do
when I'm all grown.

Vocabulary Review

Tell which word completes each sentence.

transportation
job
service
goods
volunteer
needs

1. Food and clothing and a place to live are _____.

2. Work that people do is a _____.

3. A job workers do to help others is a _____.

4. A person who works for free is a _____.

5. A plane is one type of _____.

6. Things that are grown or made are _____.

★ ★ ★ ★ ★ ★ ★ ★

Which word completes each sentence?

1. Things we would like to have are _____.

   a. goods   **b.** transportation
   c. tools   **d.** wants

Test Talk

Rule out answers you know are wrong.

2. Pliers and a hammer used by a carpenter are called _____.

   a. service   **b.** transportation
   c. tools   **d.** wants

Skills Review

Put Things in Order

Write about a job you want to do some day. Tell what you would do **first, next,** and **last.**

Follow a Route

1. What buildings are east of the store?

2. Follow the route with your finger. Where does Pat's route begin?

3. Tell what direction Pat goes on each street.

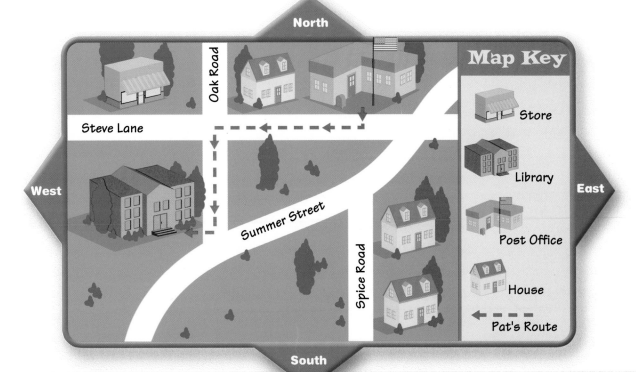

Skills Review

Use a Chart

Use the chart to answer the questions.

Tools We Used Today	
Tools	**People**
Pencil	Sara
Computer	Tony
Brush	Ryan
Ruler	Lisa

1. How many tools does the chart show?

2. Who used a ruler?

3. Who used a pencil?

Skills On Your Own

Make a chart of some jobs in your class. Write a title for your chart. Write the jobs on the left. Write the names of the helpers next to the jobs they do.

Jobs in Our Class		
	Hand out tools.	Anna
	Be line leader.	Maria
	Clean board.	Henry
	Hand out milk.	Mark

What did you learn?

1. Why do people work?

2. How are goods different from services?

3. Name some jobs. Tell what good or service each job provides.

4. **Write and Share**
   Write what you could do if you wanted to buy a toy that costs more money than you have.

Read About Work

Look for books like these in the library.

COWBOY BUNNIES
Christine Loomis
pictures by
Ora Eitan

Dancin' in the Kitchen
Illustrated by
Marjorie Priceman
Wendy Gelsanliter & Frank Christian

A Weed is a Flower
The Life of George Washington Carver
Written and illustrated by *ALIKI*

Jobs in Your Community

Make a community worker puppet. Give an interview about your community worker's job.

1 Choose a kind of worker in your community.

2 Make a puppet of your worker. Show any special clothes or tools.

3 Tell how your worker gives us goods or services.

4 Answer questions from your classmates about your worker's job.

Internet Activity

Go to www.sfsocialstudies.com/activities to learn more about people at work.

Our Earth, Our Resources

How can we care for our Earth?

Show You Care

by Julio Ortega

 Sung to the tune of "I'm a Little Teapot"

Save a lake or forest.
Show you care.
Recycle paper.
Be aware.

You can reuse boxes.
I'll show how.
Turn off water.
Reduce now!

weather

mountain

plain

lake

river

natural resource

history

Visit Our State Parks

See Plants On the Plains

Climb Bear Mountain

Hike In the Woods

Celebrate the Earth

Target Skill

Find the Main Idea

Hi! My name is Debby. My class wrote a story for the school newspaper. Every story tells about something. What the story tells about is called the **main idea.** Read our story. Find the **main idea.**

Butterfly Garden

Our class will take care of our Earth. We will plant a butterfly garden. We will plant flowers that butterflies like. We hope to have many butterfly visitors soon.

The **main idea** is in the first sentence of our newspaper story. The other sentences tell how my class will take care of the Earth.

You can use your own words to tell what a story is about. What is our newspaper story all about? It is about one way to take care of the Earth!

Try it!

Write a story about something you like to do. Then write one sentence that tells the **main idea** of your story.

Different Kinds of Weather

Today is hot.

Tomorrow my class is going to plant a butterfly garden. I can hardly wait! I hope the weather is nice. The **weather** is how it is outside at a certain place and time. I am going to check the weather report to see what tomorrow will be like.

Yesterday was warm and partly cloudy.

If tomorrow is sunny, we can plant.

If tomorrow is rainy, we can draw.

143

I live in California. My class has a pen-pal class in Michigan. Our teacher helps us e-mail them. I wonder if the weather will be warm in Michigan tomorrow.

e-mail

Hi everyone,
Tomorrow we will plant lots of brightly colored flowers. It will be hot and sunny. Some of us will ride our bikes to school. What is the weather like where you live?

Your pen pals in California

San Diego, California

Dear California pen pals,
The weather here is cold today. Yesterday was cold too. Tomorrow is supposed to be cold again. We will play in the snow at recess.

Have fun,
Your pals in Michigan

Detroit, Michigan

What did you learn?

1. How does the **weather** help you decide what to do?

2. What is the **main idea** of the letter from the class in Michigan?

3. **Think and Share** Write the words *yesterday, today,* and *tomorrow.* Draw a picture of the weather for each day. Write a sentence about each picture.

Read a Time Line

Monday **Tuesday** **Wednesday**

Debby and her class wanted to show how the weather might change during one school week. They made a time line. A **time line** shows the order in which things happen. Look at the time line. Tell how the weather changed from day to day.

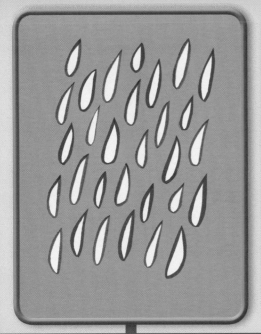

Thursday

Friday

Try it!

1. What day was it windy?

2. What was the weather like on Thursday?

3. **On Your Own** Make a **time line** about you. Draw yourself in the past, present, and in the future.

Weather and Seasons Long Ago

Long ago most children lived on farms. They did chores every day. They worked in all kinds of weather.

Milking the cow

Carrying water

Gathering firewood

148

Spring
Farmers plowed the fields and planted in the warm and rainy spring.

Summer
In the hot summer they took care of the garden and pulled the weeds.

Each Season Had Special Chores

Winter
The cold winter days were spent working indoors.

Autumn
It was time to harvest when autumn came.

What kind of chores do you do at home?
Are they different in every season?

149

Looking at Our Land and Water

Places on the Earth can have different kinds of weather. They can have different kinds of land and water too. We can do many things on land and in the water. My class is saving pictures of different kinds of land and water.

A **mountain** is the highest kind of land. It can snow and get very cold at the top of a mountain.

150

A hill is land that is higher than the land around it. A hill is not as high as a mountain. Hills have rounded tops.

A **plain** is a large piece of land. A plain is mostly flat. Plains are good for growing different kinds of food.

The ocean is the large body of salt water that covers much of our Earth.

An island is a body of land surrounded by water.

A **lake** is smaller than an ocean. Lakes have land either totally or almost totally around them.

This is a river. A **river** is a long body of water. The water in a river usually moves toward a lake or the ocean.

What did you learn?

1. How are a mountain and a plain different?

2. What kinds of land and water are near your community?

3. **Think and Share**
   Draw pictures of people doing something on land and something on water. Write a sentence about each picture.

Locate Land and Water

Debby is holding a globe. A **globe** is a round model of the Earth. You can see land and water on a globe. The blue part shows water. The rest of the globe shows land. What is Debby pointing to?

Look at a globe. Find the United States. Find your state.

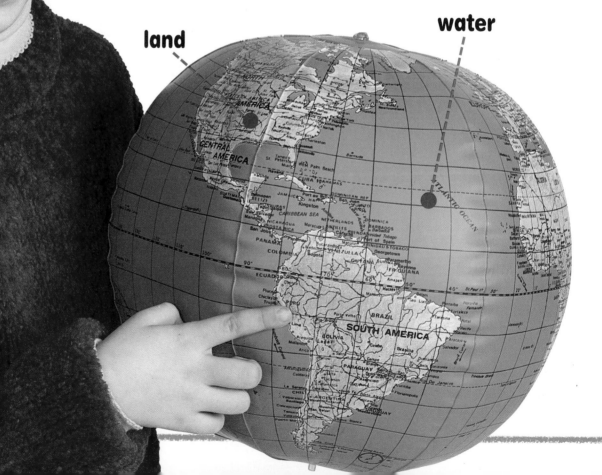

land

water

What kinds of land and water do you see on the map?

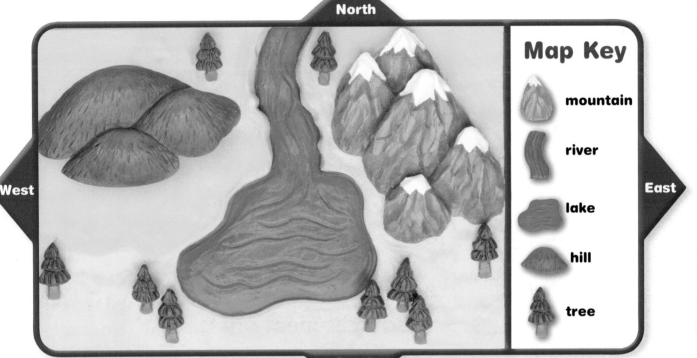

Map Key

mountain

river

lake

hill

tree

Try it!

1. What does a **globe** show? How is it like the Earth?

2. Is the river east or west of the hills?

3. **On Your Own** Look at a map of your state. Name the different kinds of land and water there.

 For more information, go online to *Atlas* at **www.sfsocialstudies.com.**

3 Our Earth's Resources

Land, water, and air are some of our Earth's natural resources. A **natural resource** is a useful thing that comes from nature.

We need land or soil to grow food. We need water to drink, cook, and wash. We also need air to breathe. All of these natural resources meet our needs.

Trees are another natural resource. Many different things can come from trees. People cut trees into lumber to build homes. They also use the fruits and nuts that grow on trees for food. Look at the pictures. What other things can come from a tree?

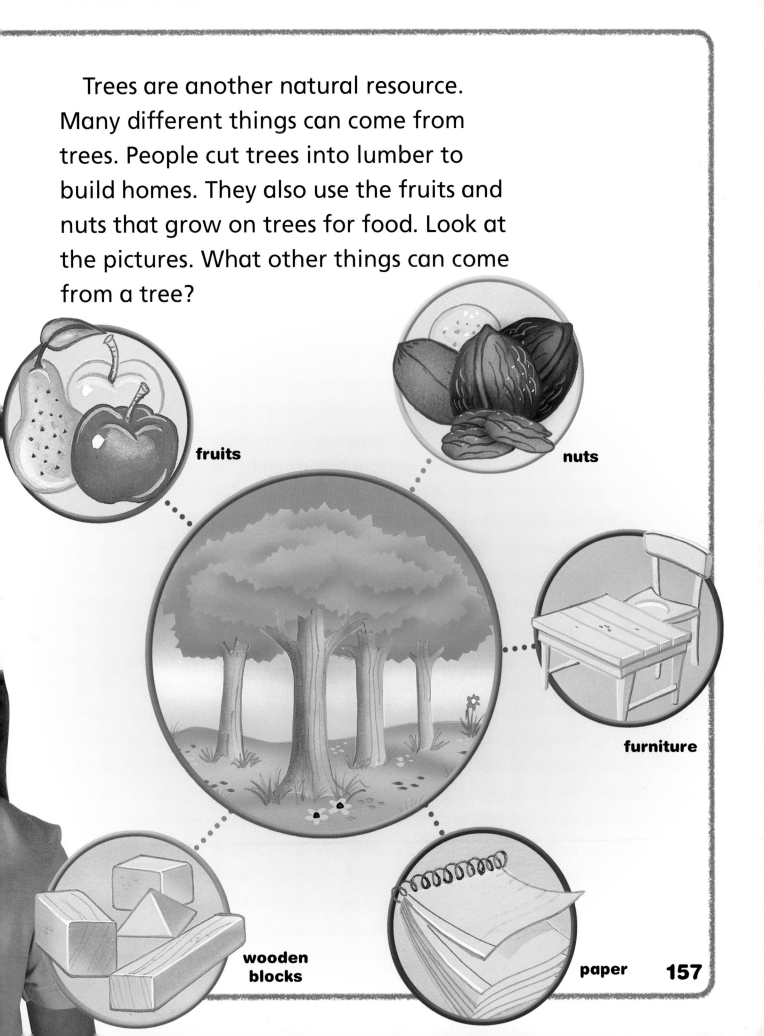

fruits

nuts

furniture

wooden blocks

paper

Oil and gas are also natural resources. They come from under the ground. They are used to heat our homes and other buildings. Some oil is made into gasoline for cars, buses, trucks, trains, and airplanes.

Oil wells get oil from the ground.

It is important to take care of our natural resources. My class wrote a report about John Muir. He wanted to help save our Earth's natural resources.

John Muir

John Muir thought natural resources were very important. He loved nature. He wrote about natural resources. He helped start many national parks.

What did you learn?

1. Name three ways **natural resources** meet our needs.

2. What is the **main idea** of the report on John Muir?

3. **Think and Share** Think about a pencil. Draw a picture of it. Name the natural resources that it came from.

Tree Musketeers is in El Segundo, California.

Tree Musketeers

Tara

When Tara was eight years old, she wanted to help take care of the Earth. Tara and a group of children planted a tree in their community.

Tara helped start a group called Tree Musketeers. Tree Musketeers has many volunteers. They take responsibility for helping the Earth. One thing they do is ask people to plant trees. Over one million trees have been planted because of Tara and Tree Musketeers!

Tree Musketeers

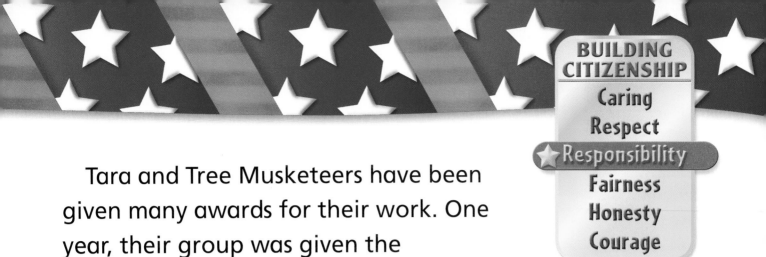

BUILDING CITIZENSHIP

Caring

Respect

⭐Responsibility

Fairness

Honesty

Courage

Tara and Tree Musketeers have been given many awards for their work. One year, their group was given the President's Volunteer Action Award.

Today, Tara Church is a young adult. She talks to young people about doing volunteer work. Tara Church thinks that volunteering is the best way to make a difference.

Tree Musketeers planting

⭐ **Responsibility in Action** ⭐

How can you be more responsible in the way you use natural resources?

161

Meet Elvia Niebla

1945–
Scientist

Elvia Niebla is a scientist
who studies forests.

Elvia was born in Mexico. When she was six years old, her family moved to Arizona. As a child, Elvia liked science. Later, Elvia Niebla went to school to learn more about trees and soil. She learned how some things might harm these natural resources. She also studied ways to protect trees and soil.

Elvia Niebla has helped write rules to protect soil. She leads scientific studies about how different materials and changes in weather can affect the soil. She knows that keeping our air and water clean can also help our forests. Elvia Niebla believes that people need to work together to protect our natural resources.

Elvia Niebla was born in Nogales, Mexico.

Think and Share

How does Elvia Niebla help take care of forests?

For more information, go online to *Meet the People* at www.sfsocialstudies.com.

Interview About Farm History

My family visits friends in Iowa. Our friends live on a farm. One day, we went to a place called "Living History Farms." **History** tells the story of people and places from the past. History also tells about things that happened in the past.

Who were the first farmers in Iowa?

164

Mrs. Waters The first farmers in Iowa were Native Americans. Native Americans called the Ioway probably farmed the land we are standing on right now!

Debby What did the Ioway grow?

Mrs. Waters They grew many things including corn, beans, pumpkins, and squash.

Mrs. Waters Many other people came to live in Iowa after the Native Americans. Some of the people who came were also farmers.

Debby What were their farms like?

Mrs. Waters Farmers grew corn, potatoes, and other food on their farms. They had oxen. These animals helped them do heavy work around the farm.

This time line shows some ways farming has changed.

1700   **1850**   **Present**

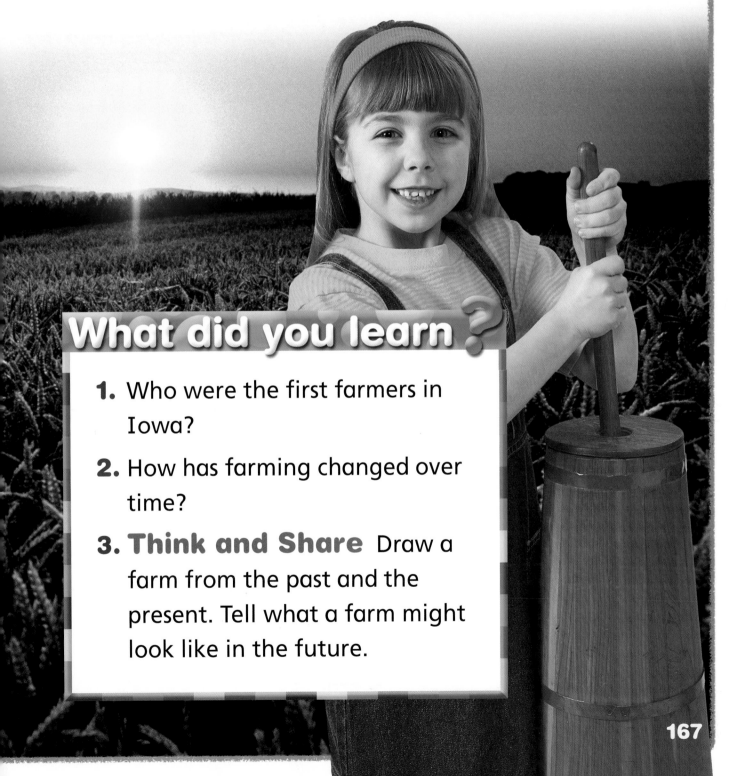

Mrs. Waters Farming continued to change over time. Some farmers began to use horses instead of oxen.

Debby Now farmers use more tools such as tractors to do farm work.

What did you learn?

1. Who were the first farmers in Iowa?

2. How has farming changed over time?

3. **Think and Share** Draw a farm from the past and the present. Tell what a farm might look like in the future.

Meet Sacagawea

about 1786–1812

Helped Lewis and Clark

Sacagawea was an important person in the history of our country. She was a Shoshone Indian who helped explorers long ago.

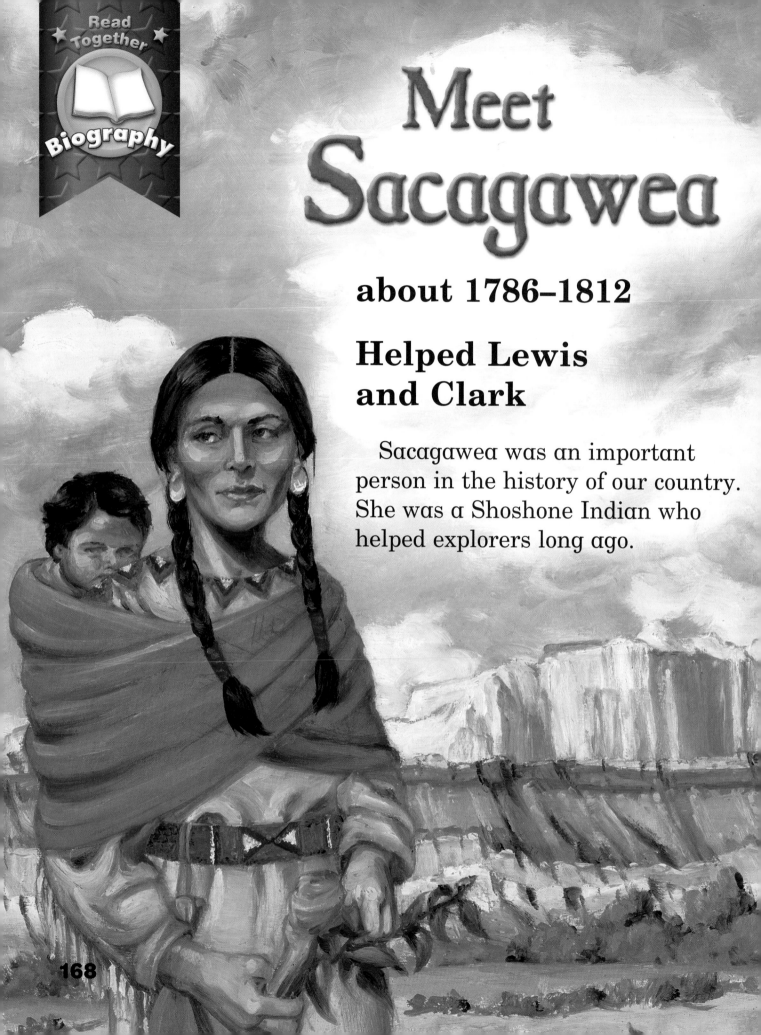

When Sacagawea was a young child, she was living in a Shoshone village in the Bitterroot Mountains in what is now Idaho. Then the Hidatsas took her to live and work in their village in what is now North Dakota.

In 1805 and 1806, a group of men was traveling across the United States. The leaders of the group were Meriwether Lewis and William Clark. They wanted to find a route to the Pacific Ocean.

Sacagawea helped Lewis and Clark on their journey. She showed them how to find food. The American Indians, or Native Americans, that Lewis and Clark met on their journey did not speak English. Sacagawea translated, or changed the words from one language to another. With the help of Sacagawea, Lewis and Clark reached the Pacific Ocean.

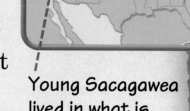

Young Sacagawea lived in what is now Idaho.

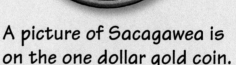

A picture of Sacagawea is on the one dollar gold coin.

Think and Share

What are two ways Sacagawea helped the explorers?

For more information, go online to *Meet the People* at **www.sfsocialstudies.com.**

169

Caring for Our Resources

Sacagawea and Lewis and Clark traveled across many different kinds of land. The land is a natural resource. Our class is learning how to help save natural resources. We follow the 3 Rs—reduce, reuse, and recycle.

Reduce! Use less paper. This will help save a tree.

Reuse! Use something again.

Please Reuse!

1. Reuse paper. Write on both sides.

2. Save bags and boxes. Reuse them.

Please Reduce!

1. Walk instead of riding in a car. This will reduce the amount of gas and oil that is used.

2. Turn off the water faucet while you brush your teeth. This will reduce the amount of water you use.

3. Turn off the light when you leave a room. This will reduce the amount of electricity you use.

We Recycle!
Paper
Cans
Plastic
Glass

Here is what our class recycles. What can you recycle at school? What can you recycle at home?

What did you learn?

1. How do you show that you care about the Earth when you reduce, reuse, and recycle?

2. What is the **main idea** of this lesson?

3. **Think and Share** In your journal, write how you can reduce, reuse, and recycle each day.

Endangered Animals

Helping the Earth helps animals too.
Some animals are endangered.

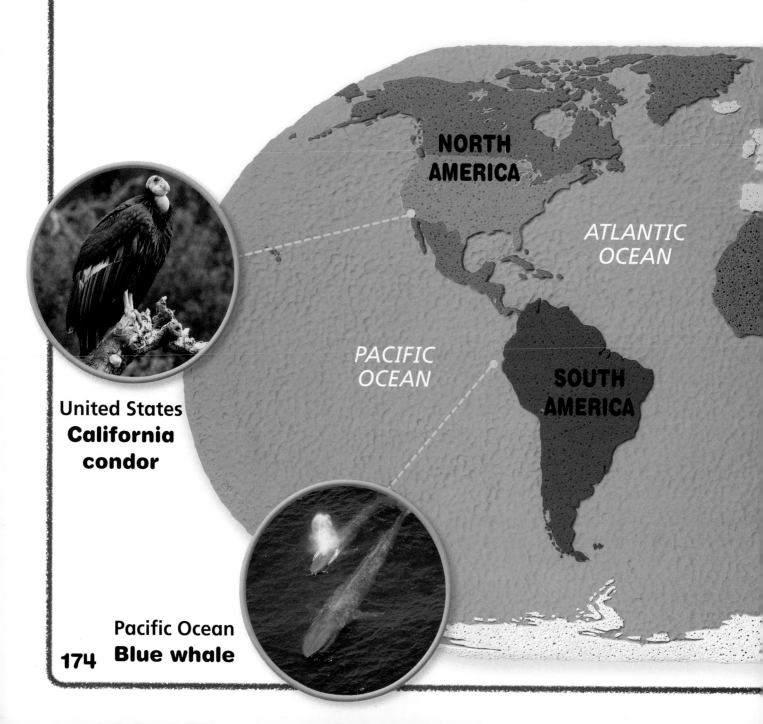

NORTH AMERICA

ATLANTIC OCEAN

PACIFIC OCEAN

SOUTH AMERICA

United States
California condor

Pacific Ocean
Blue whale

Endangered means that very few of these animals are living. Some day, some kinds of endangered animals might not be found on Earth any more. The pictures show some endangered animals.

For more information, go online to *the Atlas* at **www.sfsocialstudies.com.**

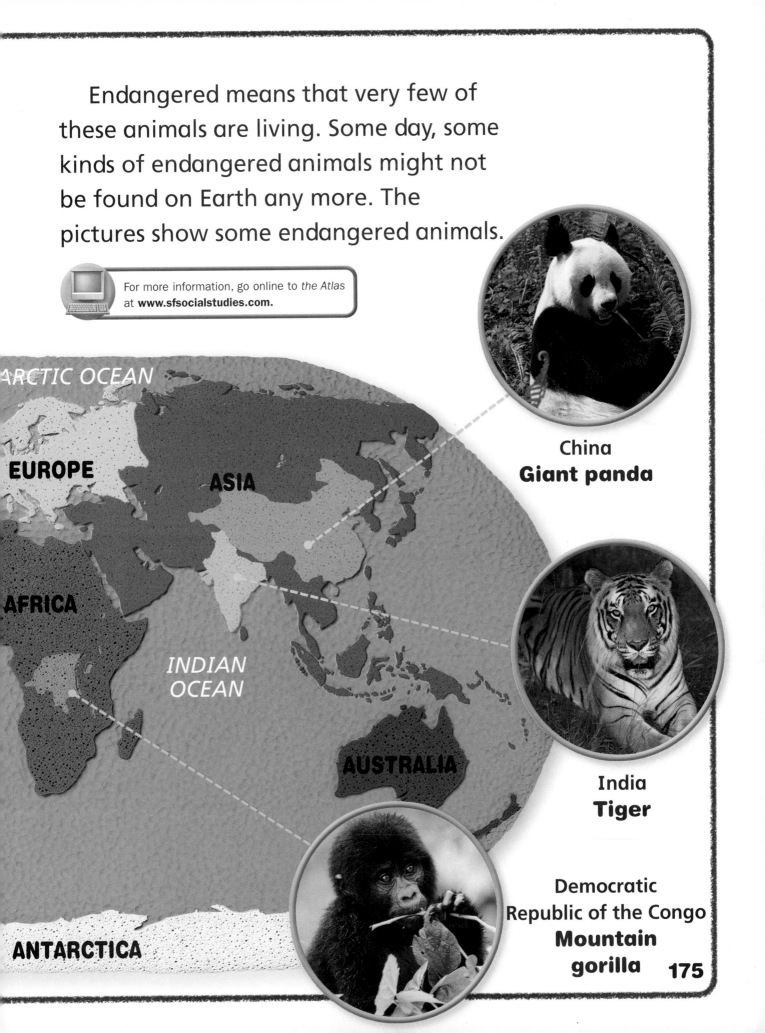

China
Giant panda

ARCTIC OCEAN

EUROPE

ASIA

AFRICA

INDIAN OCEAN

AUSTRALIA

ANTARCTICA

India
Tiger

Democratic
Republic of the Congo
**Mountain
gorilla**

End with a Legend

Johnny Appleseed

John Chapman lived many years ago. He planted so many apple seeds that people started calling him Johnny Appleseed. People have been telling stories about Johnny Appleseed for over 200 years.

Johnny grew up near an apple orchard. When he left home, he planted apple seeds wherever he went. Soon apple trees grew. Johnny Appleseed planted many apple orchards.

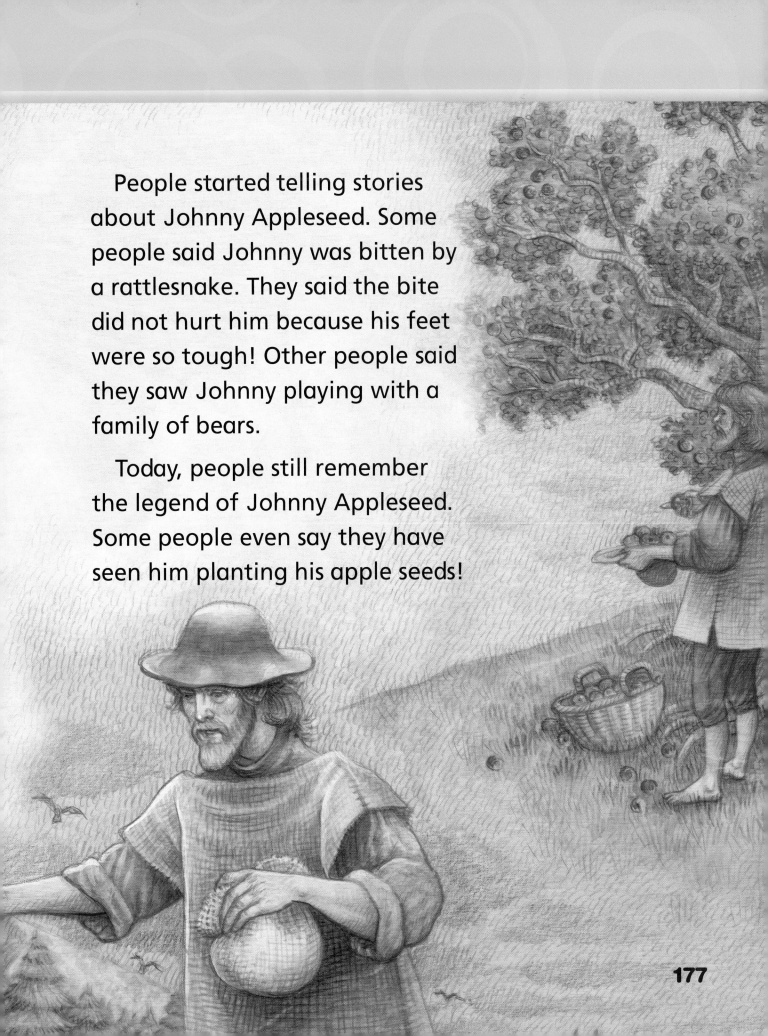

People started telling stories about Johnny Appleseed. Some people said Johnny was bitten by a rattlesnake. They said the bite did not hurt him because his feet were so tough! Other people said they saw Johnny playing with a family of bears.

Today, people still remember the legend of Johnny Appleseed. Some people even say they have seen him planting his apple seeds!

Vocabulary Review

Tell which word completes each sentence.

natural resource
river
mountain
lake

1. A useful thing that comes from the Earth is called a _____.

2. A body of water that has land around it is a _____.

3. A long body of water is called a _____.

4. The highest kind of land is a _____.

 Which word completes the sentence?

1. A story about people and places of the past is called _____.

   a. weather   **b.** recycle

   c. history   **d.** natural resource

2. Sunny is one kind of _____.

   a. mountain   **b.** weather

   c. plain   **d.** natural resource

Skills Review

Find the Main Idea

Read the following sentences.

Debby recycles each day. She saves empty cans. She saves paper after she writes or draws on it. She saves the newspaper her family reads each day. Debby and her family take the cans and paper to the recycling center in town.

What is the main idea?

a. empty cans

b. going to town

c. recycling

d. saving paper

Test Talk

Look for details to support your answer.

Locate Land and Water

Make a map and map key. Show land and water. Draw symbols on your map key. Label the symbols to show different types of land and water.

Study Skills
Read a Time Line

Debby drew a time line showing what she did each day after school. Use the time line to answer the questions.

| Monday | Tuesday | Wednesday | Thursday | Friday |

1. How many days did Debby put in her time line?

2. Which day did Debby ride her bike?

3. What did Debby do on Tuesday?

Skills On Your Own

Draw a time line of five things that happened in school this week. Write each day of the week. Draw pictures that show what happened on each day.

What did you learn?

1. Describe two kinds of weather.

2. What are some natural resources that you need to live?

3. Name three ways people can care for the Earth.

4. **Write and Share** Write about natural resources in your community. Put the **main idea** in your first sentence. Write other sentences that tell how you can use the natural resources.

Read About Earth

Look for books like these in the library.

Weather Report

Create a weather television program of your own.

1 **Choose** one kind of weather.

2 **Make** or draw something to show the weather you chose.

3 **Give** a television weather report. Show the class what you made that tells about the weather.

4 **Ask** students to tell you what they learned from your report.

Internet Activity

Go to www.sfsocialstudies.com/activities to learn more about weather.

This Is Our Country

Why is our country's past important?

Begin with a Song

Holidays Are Special Days

by LaTanya Bishop

 Sung to the tune of
"Yankee Doodle"

Holidays are special days
When families get together.
These are times we share good food
In any kind of weather!

There are times to have parades
Or have a celebration.
There are times to think about
Great people in our nation!

185

freedom

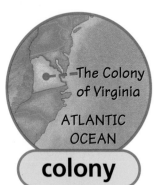

The Colony
of Virginia

ATLANTIC
OCEAN

colony

holiday

President

citizen

vote

capital

James's Story

Recall and Retell

Hi! My name is James. I wrote a story about a Seminole Indian named Little Rabbit. Read my story to find out about Little Rabbit.

Little Rabbit

Long ago there lived a boy named Little Rabbit. He liked to run races with his friends. He was very fast.

Little Rabbit was a Seminole. He lived in the Florida Everglades. Little Rabbit lived in a house called a chickee with his family. The family planted corn and other vegetables.

Little Rabbit loved to hear his grandfather tell stories. His favorite story was about a frog who could make it rain. Little Rabbit's grandfather taught him how to do the Green Corn Dance.

You **recall** when you think about something you have read or heard. You **retell** when you put it into your own words. Think about the story James wrote. Tell the story in your own words.

A Seminole family

A Seminole doll

Try it!

Draw three pictures that show something you **recall** about Little Rabbit. Use your pictures to **retell** the story in your own words.

1

Native Americans

Many different groups of Native Americans lived in North America.

The first people to live in North America were Native Americans. We also call them American Indians.

Look at the map. It shows where some Native Americans lived long ago. Today, Native Americans still live in all parts of the United States.

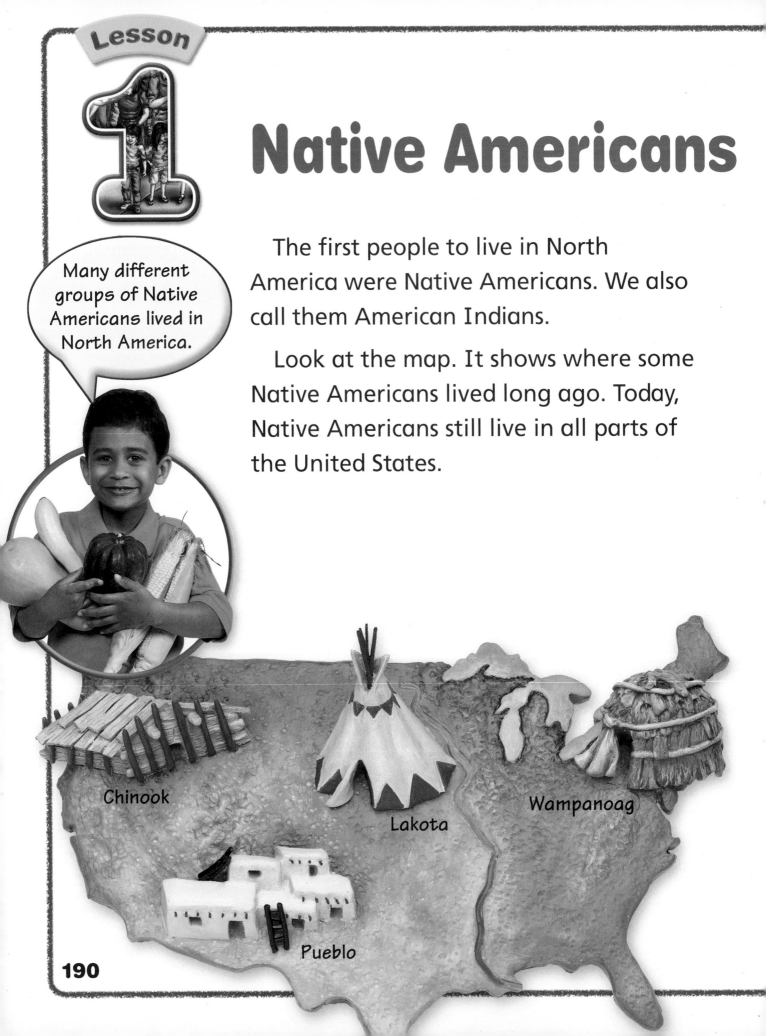

Chinook

Lakota

Wampanoag

Pueblo

Some Native American groups hunted for their food. Other groups grew food such as corn, beans, and squash. Still others caught fish.

A Pueblo home

What did you learn?

1. Who were the first people to live in North America?

2. Tell how the Pueblo home is like the Lakota home. Tell how it is different.

3. **Think and Share** Draw pictures to show three things you **recall** about Native Americans. Use your pictures to **retell** what you learned in this lesson.

Read a Diagram

Native Americans lived in different types of homes. One type of Native American home was called an earth lodge. The picture below shows an earth lodge. Native Americans made fires inside earth lodges to cook and to keep warm. Smoke from the fire left the lodge through a hole in the roof.

Look at this diagram of an earth lodge. A **diagram** shows the parts of something. Name the parts of the earth lodge you see on the diagram.

entrance

roof

hole in the roof

Try it!

1. What does a **diagram** show?

2. What part did Native Americans use to enter the earth lodge?

3. **On Your Own** Make a diagram that shows a room in your home. Label each part.

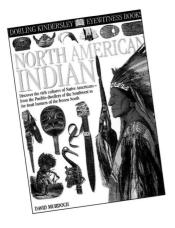

Native American Objects

Native Americans made the things they used and wore. Many of these objects are still made and used today by Native Americans in our country.

This doll is dressed in traditional Dakota clothing.

Native Americans in the Southwest have been making beautiful pottery for many years.

Colored beads forming a geometric design show the fine craftwork on this Ute child's coat.

The Penobscot are known for their deerskin moccasins, which are often decorated with colorful beads.

Tlingit women use wool from mountain goats to make dancing dresses for a special ceremony called a potlatch.

These dolls are wearing the traditional clothing worn by Seminole women.

The stick and ball game we now call Lacrosse was played by many Native American people.

Many Native Americans used cradleboards to carry their babies safely from place to place.

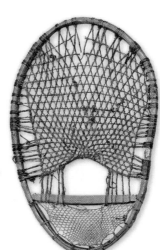

Snowshoes allowed Cree children to move more easily on different sorts of terrain and snow.

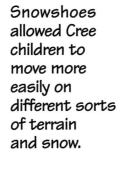

The Pomo people made fine baskets and often decorated them with feathers. The basekets were woven by both men and women.

The Nez Perce are known for their cornhusk bags.

2 Early Travelers to America

Christopher Columbus did not know about North America and the people who lived there. Long ago, Columbus sailed from Spain. Spain is a country in Europe. The king and queen of Spain told Columbus to go and find gold and other riches.

These are the names of the ships that Columbus sailed on.

North America

Santa Maria

Columbus and his crew sailed for a long time. On October 12, 1492, they landed on an island near North America. The people who lived on this island were called the Taino. Columbus did not find gold. However, he did find people and a place that other people in Europe did not know about yet.

Christopher Columbus

Every year, people remember the day Columbus landed on the island. The second Monday in October is Columbus Day.

Nina

Pinta

Spain

The Mayflower

Later, a group of people we call Pilgrims left England to come to North America. They sailed on a ship called the *Mayflower*.

The Pilgrims wanted their freedom. **Freedom** is a person's right to make choices. The Pilgrims wanted the freedom to practice their own religion.

The Pilgrims traveled far!

North America

Mayflower

England

The Pilgrims built a village that they called Plymouth. Wampanoag Indians saved the Pilgrims by showing them how to grow corn and other plants. They also showed the Pilgrims how to fish.

The Pilgrims and the Wampanoag celebrated. They were thankful. Today, people have a special day to give thanks. We call the day Thanksgiving.

What did you learn?

1. Why do we have Columbus Day and Thanksgiving?

2. Why is **freedom** important?

3. **Think and Share** Draw a picture of how Thanksgiving was celebrated long ago and how you celebrate it today. Tell how the pictures are alike and different.

Use a History Map

A history map shows places or routes from the past. Look at this map.

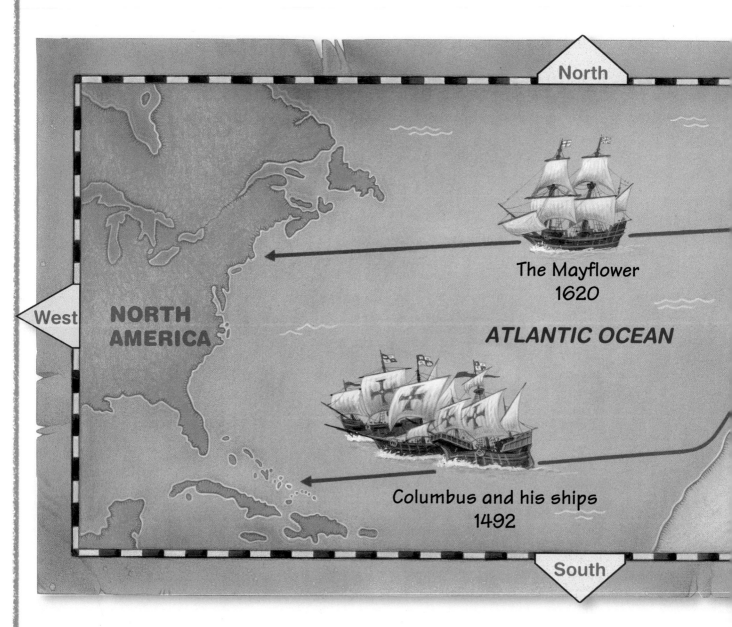

North

West

NORTH AMERICA

The Mayflower
1620

ATLANTIC OCEAN

Columbus and his ships
1492

South

Use your finger to follow the route Columbus took. Then follow the route the *Mayflower* took.

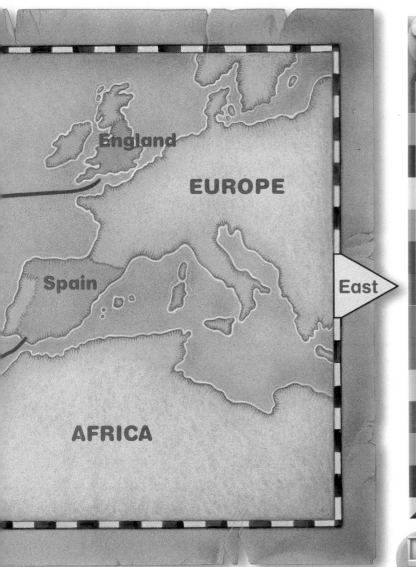

East

Try it!

1. Did Columbus sail east or west when he left Spain?

2. Name the ocean that the *Mayflower* sailed on.

3. **On Your Own** Write sentences telling what this history map shows.

For more information, go online to the *Atlas* at **www.sfsocialstudies.com**.

The Colonies Become Free

We learned that more people came to North America after the Pilgrims. They lived in places called colonies. A **colony** is a place that is ruled by a country that is far away. After a while, there were 13 colonies. These colonies were ruled by England and its king.

Williamsburg was in the colony of Virginia.

Many colonists did not want to be ruled by England. They did not want to follow England's laws. They wanted to be free. On July 4, 1776, a group of leaders in the colonies agreed on an important paper called the Declaration of Independence. In the Declaration, they wrote that everyone had the right to be free. Today, we celebrate Independence Day on July 4.

The colonies fought a war with England to be free. The war lasted many years. George Washington was a famous leader in this war. He led many battles against English soldiers.

Washington leading his soldiers

Nathan Hale was a teacher. He became a soldier in George Washington's army. He volunteered to spy on English soldiers. The English soldiers caught him. He said, "I only regret that I have but one life to lose for my country." He died in 1776.

Nathan Hale
1755-1776

General George Washington and his soldiers helped the colonies win the war against England. After the war, the colonies became a country. The country was called the United States of America.

George Washington was a hero.

What did you learn?

1. Why did many colonists want to be free?

2. Why do we celebrate Independence Day on July 4?

3. **Think and Share** Share with a classmate how each of you celebrates Independence Day. How are your celebrations alike? How are they different?

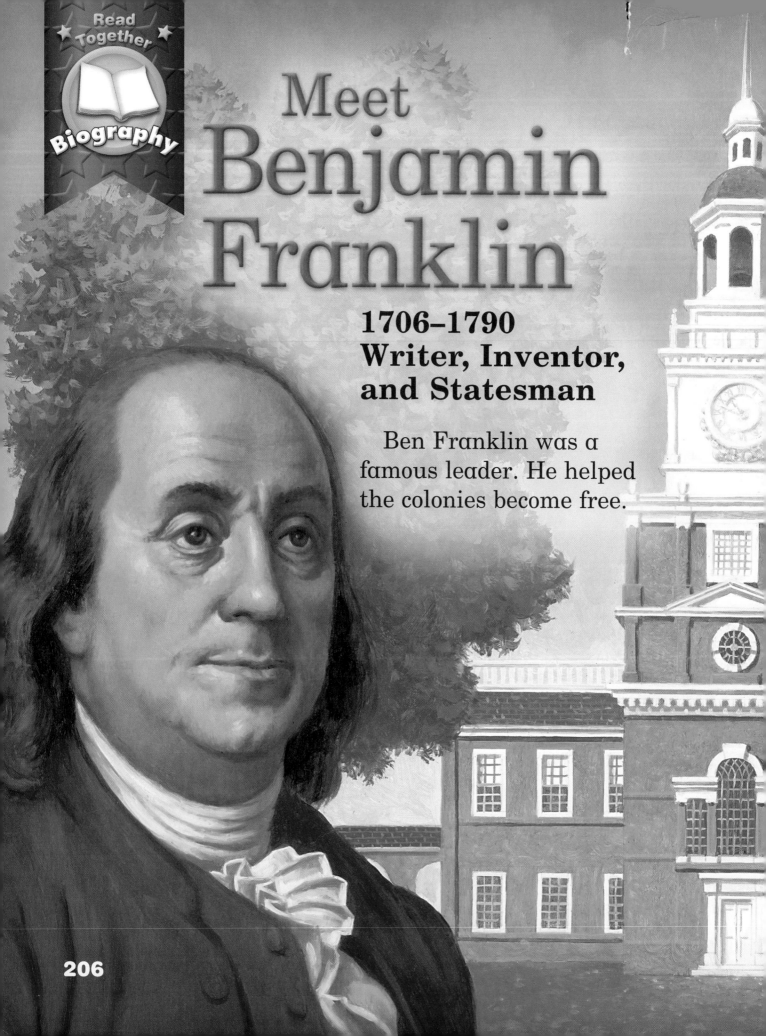

Meet Benjamin Franklin

**1706–1790
Writer, Inventor,
and Statesman**

Ben Franklin was a
famous leader. He helped
the colonies become free.

Young Ben only went to school for about two years. However, he still wanted to learn. He learned math by himself. He loved to read. When he became older, he bought his own newspaper. It became very popular.

Benjamin Franklin also wrote books. He wrote a book called *Poor Richard's Almanack*. It became very famous.

Benjamin Franklin was an inventor too. He invented the rocking chair and a special type of eyeglasses.

Benjamin Franklin wanted to help his country. He signed the Declaration of Independence. Later, he went to talk to the king of France. He asked the king to help the colonies become free. The king said he would. With France's help, America won its war against England.

Benjamin Franklin was born in Boston, Massachusetts.

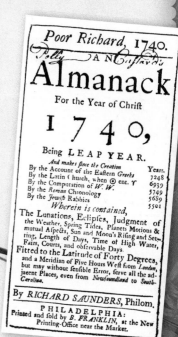

Think and Share

Why is Benjamin Franklin an important person in our country's history?

For more information, go online to *Meet the People* at **www.sfsocialstudies.com**.

Symbols in Our Country

The Statue of Liberty stands for hope and freedom.

We have many different symbols in our country.

The Washington Monument honors George Washington.

The Liberty Bell stands for freedom.

Picture	Diagram

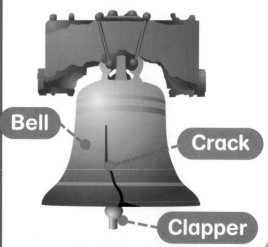

Bell

Crack

Clapper

208

The Capitol Building is in Washington, D.C. It is where the leaders of our country meet.

Our country's motto is "In God We Trust." A motto is a saying that people try to live by. Our country's motto stands for freedom and trust.

The bald eagle was named our country's bird in 1782.

Uncle Sam is a symbol for the United States of America

What did you learn?

1. What can symbols stand for?

2. Look at the diagram of the Liberty Bell. What part is inside the bell?

3. **Think and Share** Draw a new symbol for our country. Tell what your symbol stands for.

Our Country's Flag

Our country's flag is a famous symbol of freedom. Look at the pictures. They show some ways our flag has changed from the past to the present.

Today, the stripes stand for the number of states our country had when it became free. The 50 stars stand for each of our 50 states.

1776   1795

Our flag today

Hands-on History

Draw a picture of a place where you have seen our country's flag flying.

1818

1912-1959

211

5

We Celebrate Holidays

We fly the United States flag on many holidays. A **holiday** is a special day. We celebrate some holidays to honor important people. We celebrate other holidays to honor something important that happened in our country's history.

Independence Day celebration

Memorial Day and Veterans Day are two holidays. On these days, Americans honor the people who fought in our country's wars.

Memorial Day celebration

HONORING VETERANS 34
Continuing to Serve
©2001 USPS

Veterans Day celebration

Martin Luther King, Jr. Day is in January. On this holiday, we honor Martin Luther King, Jr.

Dr. King believed that all people should have the right to be treated fairly. He worked hard so that African Americans would be treated with respect. He wanted all Americans to be treated the same. His birthday was on January 15.

We celebrate Presidents' Day in February. The **President** is our country's leader. We honor George Washington and Abraham Lincoln on this holiday. Both of these Presidents were born in February.

George Washington was our country's first President. We call him the "Father of our Country."

George Washington

Abraham Lincoln

What did you learn?

1. Why are Memorial Day and Veterans Day important **holidays**?

2. Why do we celebrate Martin Luther King, Jr. Day?

3. **Write and Share** Tell why we celebrate holidays.

Meet Abraham Lincoln

1809–1865
United States President

Abraham Lincoln was known as "Honest Abe." He was the 16th President of the United States.

Young Abe's family was very poor. He was not sent to school very often. However, he taught himself many different things. He liked to read books and tell stories. People liked listening to him. They thought he was a good speaker. Abraham Lincoln worked hard and became a lawyer. Later he became President of the United States.

Abraham Lincoln was the leader of our country during a war between the states. The states were fighting for many reasons. One reason was because some states wanted African Americans to be free. Other states did not. Abraham Lincoln worked to keep our country together. He helped free African Americans.

Abraham Lincoln was born near Hodgenville, Kentucky.

Lincoln's hat

Lincoln's home when he was a boy

Think and Share

Why is Abraham Lincoln remembered as one of our greatest Presidents?

For more information, go online to *Meet the People* at **www.sfsocialstudies.com**.

6 Choosing Our Country's Leaders

I am a citizen of the United States. A **citizen** is a member of a state and country. Adult citizens of the United States have the right to vote for their leaders. A **vote** is a choice that gets counted.

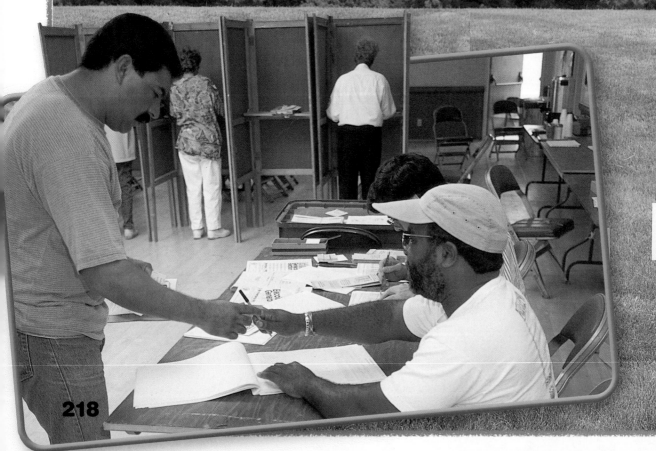

Make A Difference

Each citizen votes one time. When the voting is finished, each vote is counted. Whoever gets the most votes, wins.

Vote For Governor

I Voted Today

VOTE For Our President

VOTE NOW

Re-ELECT Our Mayor

Your Vote Counts

Every state has a leader called a governor. Citizens of each state vote for their governor. The governor works with other state leaders to help make laws for their state.

Each state has a capital. A **capital** is the city where important leaders of a state or country live and work. What is your state's capital? Find it on a map.

The governor of Georgia works in Atlanta.

Our country also has a capital. It is called Washington, D.C. The President of the United States lives and works in our country's capital.

The President works with other leaders in our country to help make our country's laws. Citizens vote for President every four years in our country.

Washington D.C. is the capital of the United States.

What did you learn?

1. How does a person's **vote** help decide who will be leader?

2. Who is the leader of our state? Who is the leader of our country?

3. **Think and Share Recall** three things you learned about the President of the United States. **Retell** what you learned.

Eleanor Roosevelt

Eleanor Roosevelt was born in New York City, New York.

When Eleanor was young, she was very shy. When she grew older, she became more comfortable around people. She married a man named Franklin Roosevelt. He became our 32nd President.

Eleanor Roosevelt saw that there were problems in our country. She told people the truth about what she saw. She helped the poor. She worked hard to get equal rights for all people.

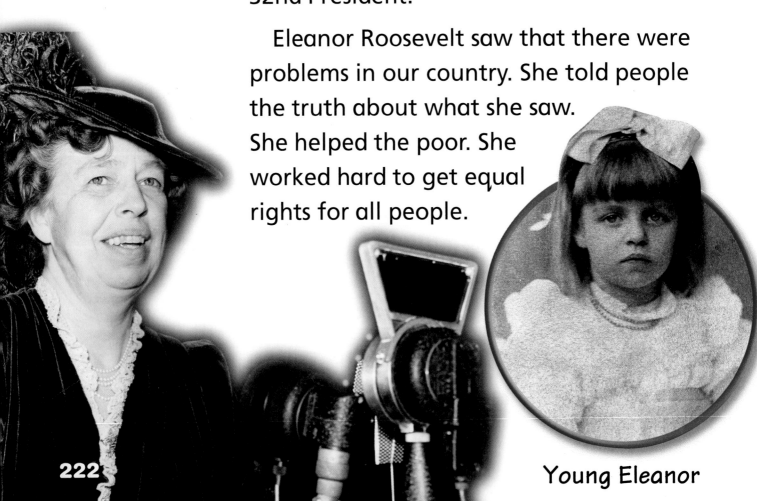

Young Eleanor

BUILDING
CITIZENSHIP
Caring
Respect
Responsibility
Fairness
★ Honesty
Courage

Eleanor Roosevelt wrote many books and newspaper articles. She was honest. She would say and write what she thought.

Eleanor Roosevelt traveled around the world many times. She visited many countries. She met many of the world's leaders.

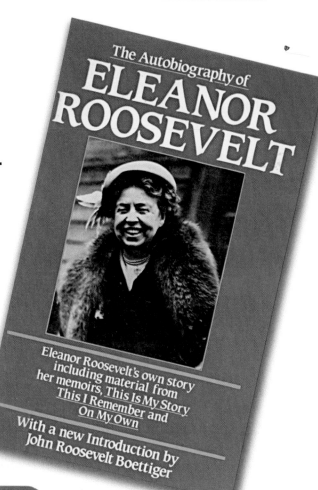

The Autobiography of
ELEANOR ROOSEVELT

Eleanor Roosevelt's own story including material from her memoirs, This Is My Story, This I Remember and On My Own

With a new Introduction by John Roosevelt Boettiger

 Honesty in Action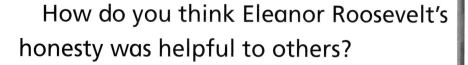

How do you think Eleanor Roosevelt's honesty was helpful to others?

The Star-Spangled Banner
by Francis Scott Key

Oh, say! can you see,
by the dawn's early light,

What so proudly we hailed
at the twilight's last gleaming?

Whose broad stripes and bright stars,
through the perilous fight,

O'er the ramparts we watched
were so gallantly streaming?

And the rockets' red glare,
the bombs bursting in air,

Gave proof through the night
that our flag was still there.

O say, does that Star-Spangled
Banner yet wave

O'er the land of the free
and the home of the brave?

Vocabulary Review

Match each word to a picture.

vote
holiday
President
capital

1.

2.

3.

4.

★ ★ ★ ★ ★ ★ ★ ★

 TEST PREP Which word completes the sentence?

1. The Pilgrims came to North America for _____.

   a. a holiday   **b.** riches

   c. freedom   **d.** gold

2. A member of a state and country is called a _____.

   a. citizen   **b.** capital

   c. holiday   **d.** vote

Skills Review

◎ Recall and Retell

Make a list of what you learned about Nathan Hale. Read your list. Then put the list away. Try to **recall** what the list said and **retell** what you remember to a friend.

Use a History Map

Ben Franklin traveled to France in 1776. Look at the map to answer these questions.

1. Which direction did Ben Franklin travel to France?

2. What ocean did he travel across?

3. What continent is south of France?

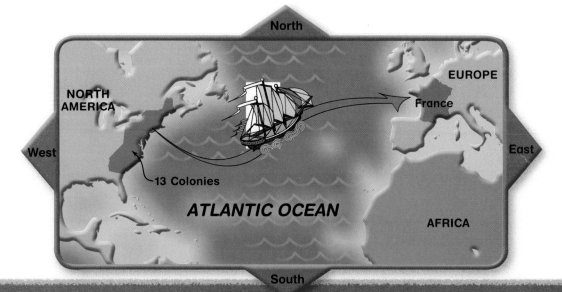

Study Skills
Read a Diagram

Look at the diagram of the Statue of Liberty. Answer the questions.

1. What is the highest part of the statue?

2. What part is on the statue's head?

3. Where can you stand to look down at the ground?

Skills On Your Own

Draw a diagram of the front of a penny. Label the parts. What President of the United States is pictured on the penny?

Test Talk

Use the diagram to help you find the answer.

Torch

Crown

Lookout

What did you learn?

1. Tell what the United States flag and the Liberty Bell stand for.

2. Name three important Americans we honor with a holiday.

3. What does a governor do?

4. **Write and Share** Write about some of the reasons why you are proud to be an American or living in the United States.

Read About Our Country

Look for books like these in the library.

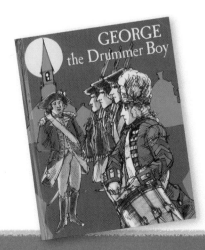

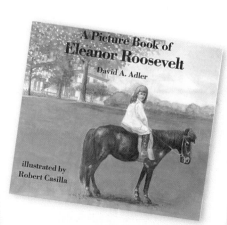

UNIT 5 Project

History on Parade

Have a history parade.

1 Choose something that happened in the past.

2 Draw or make an object that shows what happened.

3 Tell what happened.

4 Line up in order of when things happened. The first event should be first in line. The last event should be last. Walk around your classroom on parade.

Internet Activity

Go to www.sfsocialstudies.com/activities to learn more about American history.

Our Country, Our World

UNIT 6

Where in the world would you like to visit?

231

Explore with Me!

by Sylvia Chang

 Sung to the tune of "Hush, Little Baby"

Travel the world. Explore with me.
There are so many things to do and see.
There are people we will meet.
There are new foods we will eat.

We'll take a boat, a bus, and train.
We'll fly around the world in a great big plane.
We'll learn many things we want to know.
We'll tell all about each place we go.

market

communicate

invention

inventor

world

UNIT
6

Kay's Grandparents

Target Skill

Predict

Hi. My name is Kay. My grandparents just arrived for a visit. They have traveled to many countries. They brought me gifts from some of the countries. They brought me a fan from Japan. They also brought me clothes and other gifts from Mexico and stuffed animals from Australia.

236

Now I want to give my grandparents a gift. I can draw a picture for them. I can make a card. I can give them flowers.

It is time to predict. **Predict** means to tell what you think will happen next. What do you think I will give my grandparents?

I decided to draw them a picture of myself. They said they liked it very much. Did I do what you thought I would do?

Try it!

The sky is very dark and cloudy. **Predict** what kind of weather you might have.

1

Visiting the Market

Tomorrow is Grandparents Day at my school! Many grandparents will come to visit. They will bring special foods to our class.

My grandparents and I went to the market to buy the food we will bring. A **market** is a place where goods are sold.

238

People who work at the market provide services. One worker weighed the vegetables we picked out.

My grandmother said she went to the market every day with her mother and grandmother. They bought food for the family.

What did you learn

1. What goods did Kay and her grandparents buy?

2. What service did they use?

3. Kay and her grandparents chose their groceries. They took the groceries to the front of the store. **Predict** what may happen next.

Gather Information

Kay's class had to find out about people long ago. Kay went to the museum with her grandparents. She learned about other countries. Kay and her grandparents bought picture cards that told about some important leaders who lived long ago.

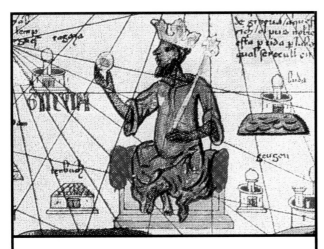

Mansa Musa

West Africa

Mansa Musa was the ruler of a country in West Africa called Mali.

Cleopatra

Egypt

Cleopatra became the queen of Egypt when she was only eighteen years old.

Augustus Caesar

Rome

Augustus Caesar was the leader of many lands. He made laws that were fair to all people.

Kublai Khan

China

Kublai Khan was a powerful ruler in China. He believed in treating people fairly.

Try it!

1. How are these leaders alike and different?

2. Name other ways to gather information about people who lived long ago.

3. **On Your Own** Tell or write an interesting fact about each of these people.

How Things Have Changed

We learned many interesting things from the grandparents who visited our class. They told us how work has changed. We learned how some things at home have changed too.

I used a typewriter. Now people use computers!

I used to punch buttons at the store. Now I scan.

My class made a chart to show other ways things have changed. How do you think things might change in the future?

Object					
How It Has Changed					

What did you learn?

1. Tell two ways work has changed.

2. How has something you do for fun changed?

3. **Think and Share** Think of something you use at home. **Predict** how it might change in the future. Draw a picture and write or tell about it.

Joseph Bruchac was born in Saratoga Springs, New York.

Joseph Bruchac

Joseph lived with his grandparents when he was young. Joseph's grandfather was an Abenaki Indian.

Joseph became interested in the stories told by Native American, or American Indian, elders. Many of the stories told how we should respect each other and the Earth.

BUILDING CITIZENSHIP

Caring
★ Respect
Responsibility
Fairness
Honesty
Courage

Today, Joseph Bruchac is a writer. He still listens to stories told by Native American elders. He tells these stories in many of his books and poems. He also sings songs. Many of the songs tell Native American stories.

Joseph Bruchac respects Native American stories. He thinks it is a good idea to share these stories. He thinks people can learn a lot from them.

★ Respect in Action ★

How does Joseph Bruchac show that he respects Native American stories?

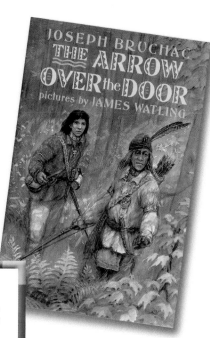

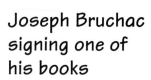

Joseph Bruchac signing one of his books

245

Inventors and Inventions

Telling stories and singing songs are two ways to communicate. You **communicate** when you give and get information.

An **invention** is something new. Many inventions have helped people communicate. The printing press and the telephone are two important inventions people have used to communicate.

Long ago, there were no machines to copy the pages of a book. Books had to be copied by hand. This took a long time. Then an inventor made a machine called the printing press. An **inventor** is someone who makes or invents something new.

People could use the printing press to make many copies of a page. Books and newspapers could be made more quickly. People in many places around the world were able to get information from the books and newspapers.

Johannes Gutenberg was the inventor of the printing press.

First printing press

A man named Alexander Graham Bell invented the telephone. With a telephone, people did not have to be in the same room to talk to each other. They could use the telephone to talk to someone miles away. The telephone helped change the way people communicate.

Alexander Graham Bell

1847–1922

Alexander Graham Bell taught at a school for the deaf. He helped start the first telephone company called Bell Telephone Company.

Thomas Alva Edison

1847–1931

Thomas Edison made more than 1,000 inventions. Many of his inventions helped people communicate better. He also invented many other things, such as the light bulb we use today.

Thomas Alva Edison was a famous inventor. One of his inventions was the phonograph. This was the first time people could hear recorded sounds. What do you use to hear recorded sounds?

Today, people around the world communicate in many ways. We even have machines that let people on Earth talk to astronauts in space!

A phonograph from long ago

What did you learn?

1. Why are Edison and Bell such important **inventors**?

2. How did Alexander Graham Bell change the way people **communicate**?

3. **Think and Share** Recall and retell what you learned about Thomas Alva Edison.

Telephones

Alexander Graham Bell makes a telephone call.

Alexander Graham Bell invented the telephone in 1876. How do telephones help people?

Bell's "Box telephone" of 1876–1877 had a combined mouthpiece and earpiece.

Mouthpiece and earpiece combined

Earpiece

In early years, an operator took your number and the number you wanted. Then the operator connected the call.

The first telephone wires were copper with a glass covering.

This wall phone of 1879 was invented by Thomas Edison.

Mouthpiece

By 1885, the mouthpiece and earpiece were combined to form a handset.

Earpiece

"Cradle" telephones like this one were popular by the 1890s. This phone is from 1937.

Hook for earpiece

Earpiece

Mouthpiece

Numbered dial

How Travel Has Changed

Horse and Wagon

Bicycle

The way people communicate has changed. The way people travel has also changed. The time line shows some ways transportation on land has changed from the past to the present.

252

Old Model T Car

Car of Today

What did you learn ?

1. How has the way we travel on land changed?

2. Name other ways people can travel on land.

3. **Think and Share** **Predict** how people might drive in the future. Draw a picture and tell about it.

Read a Bar Graph

A **bar graph** helps you compare groups. Look at this bar graph. The title is at the top of the graph. The pictures on the side of the graph show how Kay's class thinks children will travel to school in the future.

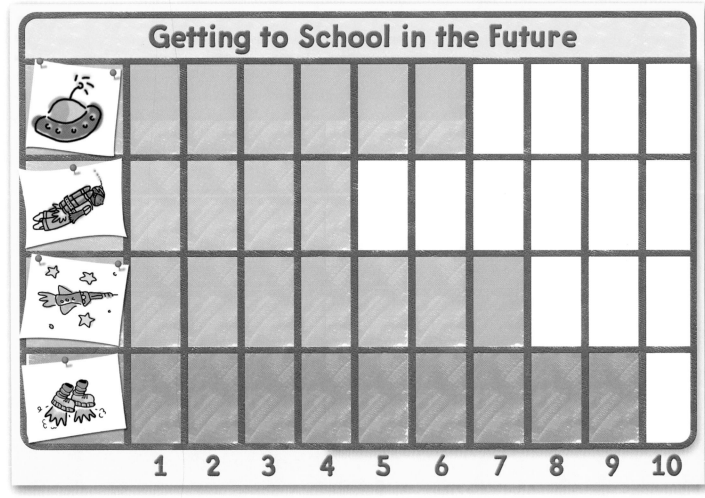

Getting to School in the Future

1   2   3   4   5   6   7   8   9   10

Use your finger to follow the bar next to the rocket. Find the number at the bottom of the graph. It shows that seven children think people will travel to school by rocket in the future.

Try it!

1. What is the title of the **bar graph**?

2. How does Kay's class think most children will travel to school in the future?

3. **On Your Own** Make a bar graph with your class of favorite ways to travel. Predict what most of your class will choose.

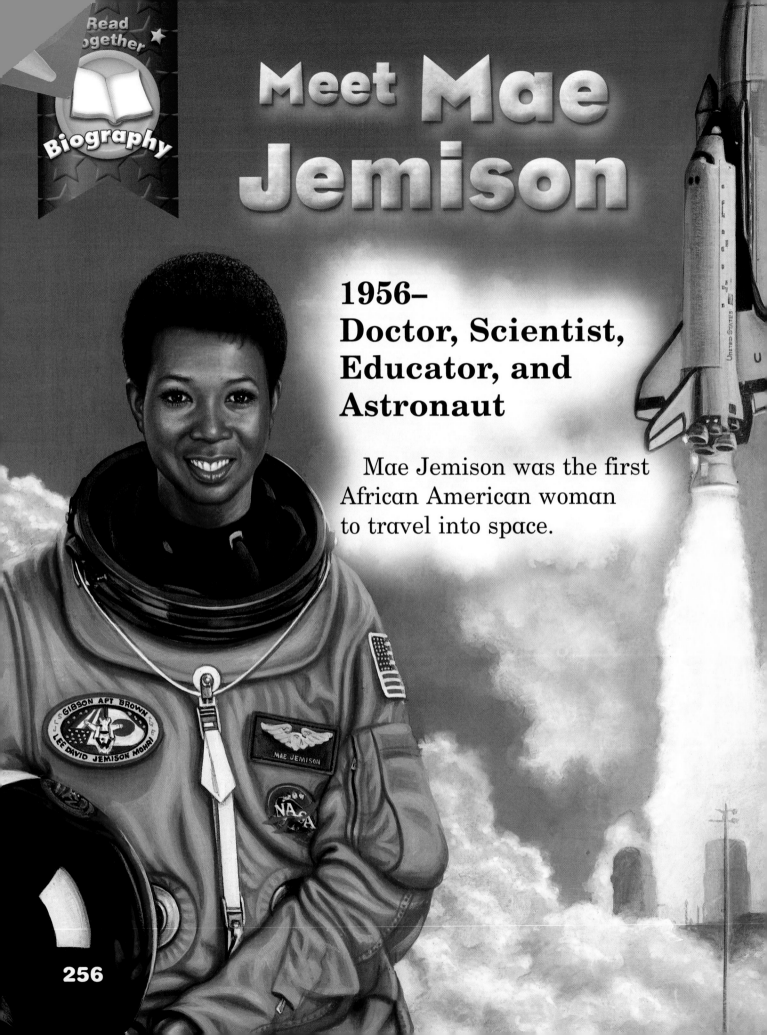

Meet Mae Jemison

1956–
Doctor, Scientist, Educator, and Astronaut

Mae Jemison was the first African American woman to travel into space.

Mae liked science when she was a child. She grew up to become a doctor and scientist. Mae Jemison traveled many places around the world. She helped to care for the people living in each place.

Later, Mae Jemison joined the NASA Space Program. She was the science mission specialist on the space shuttle *Endeavour*. In space, she helped do many experiments. Some of these experiments looked at how being in space affected people and animals.

After she left NASA, Mae Jemison started a group that works on many different projects. The group started a science camp for children. The camp is called The Earth We Share. At the camp, children from around the world learn about science.

Mae Jemison was born in Decatur, Alabama.

Mae Jemison working in space

Think and Share

Think about something that interests you. Tell what jobs you might do using your interest.

For more information, go online to *Meet the People* at **www.sfsocialstudies.com**.

Life Around the World

The world looks different from way up in space.

From space, Dr. Jemison could look down at the world. The **world** is a name for Earth and everything on it. Look at the picture. It shows how the world looks from space.

From space, everything on the world might look like it is the same. When you are closer, you can see how people around the world are alike and different. Look at the pictures of children around the world. How is the clothing they wear like what you wear? How is it different?

My name is Mónika. I live in Hungary.

My name is Carlitos. I live in Argentina.

My name is Esta. I live in Tanzania.

My name is Daisuke. I live in Japan.

What people eat and where they live can be alike and different too. The chart shows different food and homes from around the world.

Child	 Mónika Hungary
Favorite Food	meat and vegetable soup
Home	

260

the World

Carlitos
Argentina

Esta
Tanzania

Daisuke
Japan

sausage

beans

rice cakes wrapped
in seaweed

What did you learn?

1. How are homes around the world alike and different?

2. What does Carlitos eat? How is it different from what Mónika eats?

3. **Think and Share**
   How are these children like you?

Meet Laurence Yep

1948– Author

Many of Laurence Yep's books tell about Chinese American people.

Laurence Yep is Chinese American. He grew up in California. He went to school in a part of San Francisco called Chinatown. Many of the children at his school spoke Chinese. Laurence spoke English.

Later, Laurence Yep started writing books. He became very interested in the Chinese American way of life. Many of his books are set in Chinese American places such as Chinatown.

Laurence Yep writes books for both children and young adults. His books have won many awards. His books *DragonWings* and *Dragon's Gate* have both won an important award called the Newbery Medal.

Laurence Yep was born in San Francisco, California.

The Newbery Medal

Think and Share

What can we learn when we read about people around the world?

 For more information, go online to *Meet the People* at **www.sfsocialstudies.com**.

It Is Time to Leave

People around the world are alike and different in many ways.

Good-bye

United States

NORTH AMERICA

Adios

Bolivia

PACIFIC OCEAN

ATLANTIC OCEAN

SOUTH AMERICA

Adeus

Au revoir

264

Brazil

France

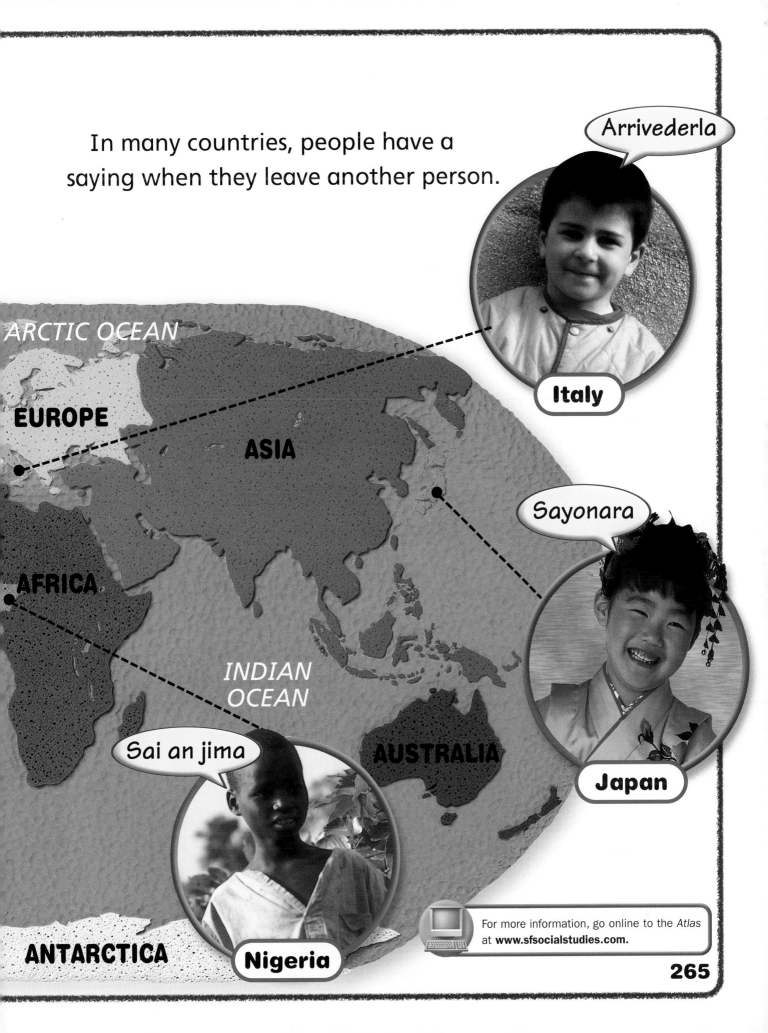

In many countries, people have a saying when they leave another person.

Arrivederla

Italy

Sayonara

Japan

Sai an jima

Nigeria

ARCTIC OCEAN

EUROPE

ASIA

AFRICA

INDIAN OCEAN

AUSTRALIA

ANTARCTICA

For more information, go online to the *Atlas* at **www.sfsocialstudies.com**.

265

The Girl and the Milk Pail

Adapted from Aesop

One day, a little girl went to milk the cow. While she milked, she thought, "I want new clothes." She carried the bucket of milk on her head as she walked home.

The little girl began to think. First, she thought about how she would sell the milk at the market. With the money she made, she could buy eggs.

After that, she would feed the chickens that hatched from the eggs. Then she would take the chickens to the market. Finally, she could buy new clothes!

She could not wait. She began to run home. She thought, "How beautiful I will look in my new clothes." She could not hold on to the bucket. It fell off her head! All of the milk spilled out.

Moral: Sometimes when you hurry, you only get farther behind.

Vocabulary Review

world
inventor
market

Tell which word completes each sentence.

1. Thomas Edison was a famous _____.

2. A place to buy goods is called a _____.

3. The Earth and everything on it is called the _____.

★ ★ ★ ★ ★ ★ ★ ★

 Which word completes the sentence?

1. You give and get information when you _____.

   a. market   **b.** inventor

   c. communicate   **d.** world

2. The telephone was an important _____.

   a. inventor   **b.** invention

   c. market   **d.** world

Skills Review

Predict

In your class, vote for your favorite pet. **Predict** which pet will get the most votes.

★ ★ ★ ★ ★ ★ ★ ★

Gather Information

Suppose you want to gather information about a topic. The library is a good place to start. Books, encyclopedias, newspapers, and the Internet can help you find what you are looking for. Choose one of the people from the list below. Decide if you will use a book, encyclopedia, newspaper, or the Internet to help you learn about that person. Write one sentence about the person you chose.

1. Thomas Jefferson
2. Betsy Ross
3. Martin Luther King, Jr.
4. Neil Armstrong
5. Sally Ride
6. Bill Gates

Skills Review
Read a Bar Graph

Kay asked her friends to name their favorite color. Read her bar graph to answer the questions.

1. How many friends did Kay ask?

2. What color did the most people like?

3. What color did three people like?

Our Favorite Colors

	1	2	3	4	5
Blue					
Pink					
Green					
Purple					

Skills On Your Own

Make a bar graph that shows how you and some friends travel to school. Ask your friends how they get to school. Write the ways they get to school on the left. Write numbers on the bottom. Fill in the bar to show how many travel in each way.

What did you learn?

1. What goods and services can you get in a market?

2. Name two inventors who helped change the way people communicate.

3. Name three ways people can be alike and different.

4. **Write and Share** Write about how one thing people use at home has changed.

Test Talk

Is your answer complete and correct?

Read About Our World

Look for books like these in the library.

TRAIN SONG

by HARRIET ZIEFERT · paintings by DONALD SAAF

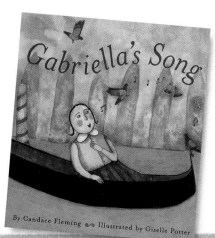

Gabriella's Song

By Candace Fleming ✤ Illustrated by Giselle Potter

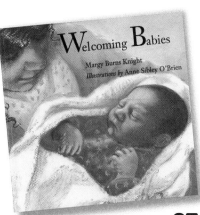

Welcoming Babies

Margy Burns Knight

Illustrations by Anne Sibley O'Brien

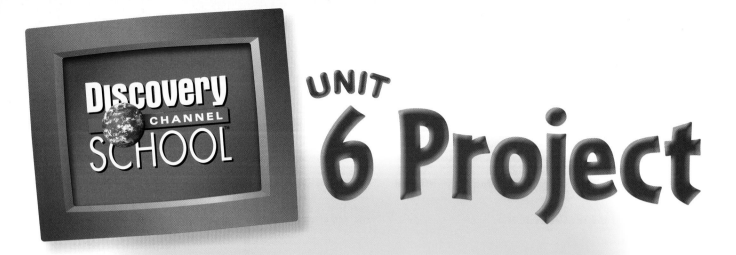
Future World

Invent a machine of the future.

1 **Think** of a machine people might use in the future.

2 **Make** a model of your machine.

3 **Give** a commercial. Tell why people should use your machine.

4 **Ask** your classmates if they would or wouldn't use your machine and why.

Internet Activity

Go to www.sfsocialstudies.com/activities to learn more about inventions.

Table of Contents

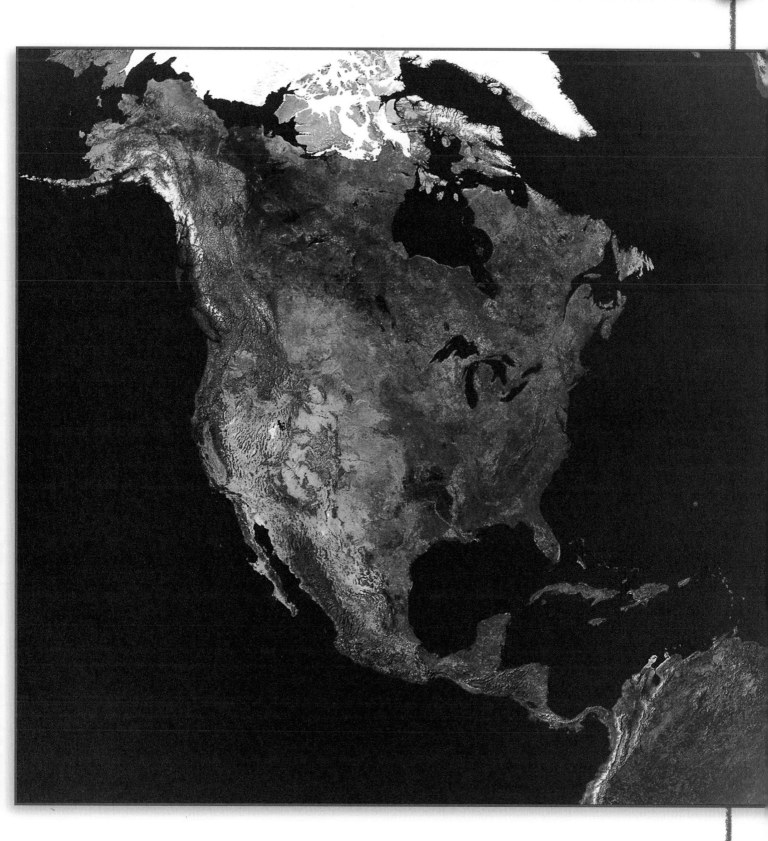

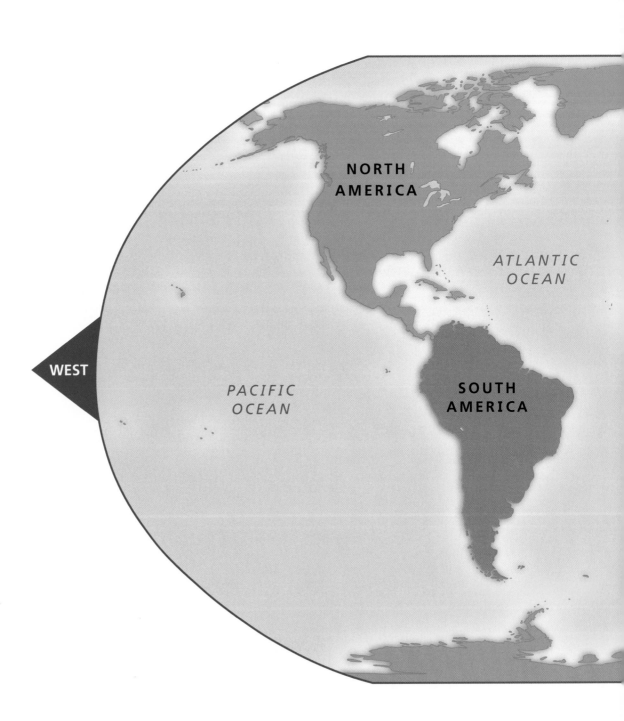

WEST

NORTH
AMERICA

ATLANTIC
OCEAN

PACIFIC
OCEAN

SOUTH
AMERICA

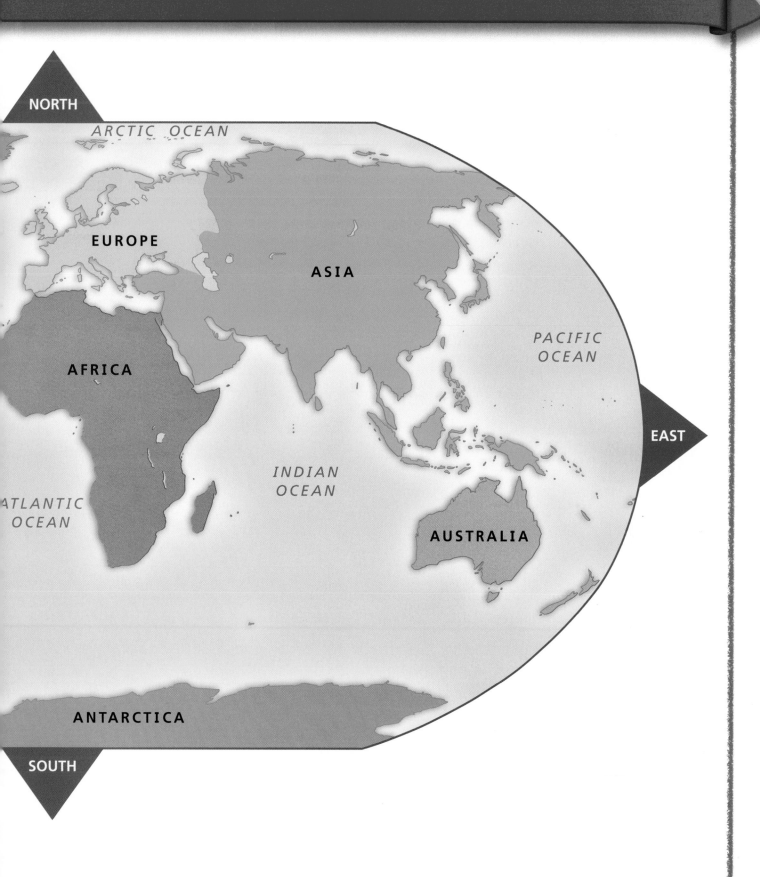

NORTH

ARCTIC OCEAN

EUROPE

ASIA

PACIFIC OCEAN

AFRICA

EAST

ATLANTIC OCEAN

INDIAN OCEAN

AUSTRALIA

ANTARCTICA

SOUTH

Atlas

Map of the United States of America

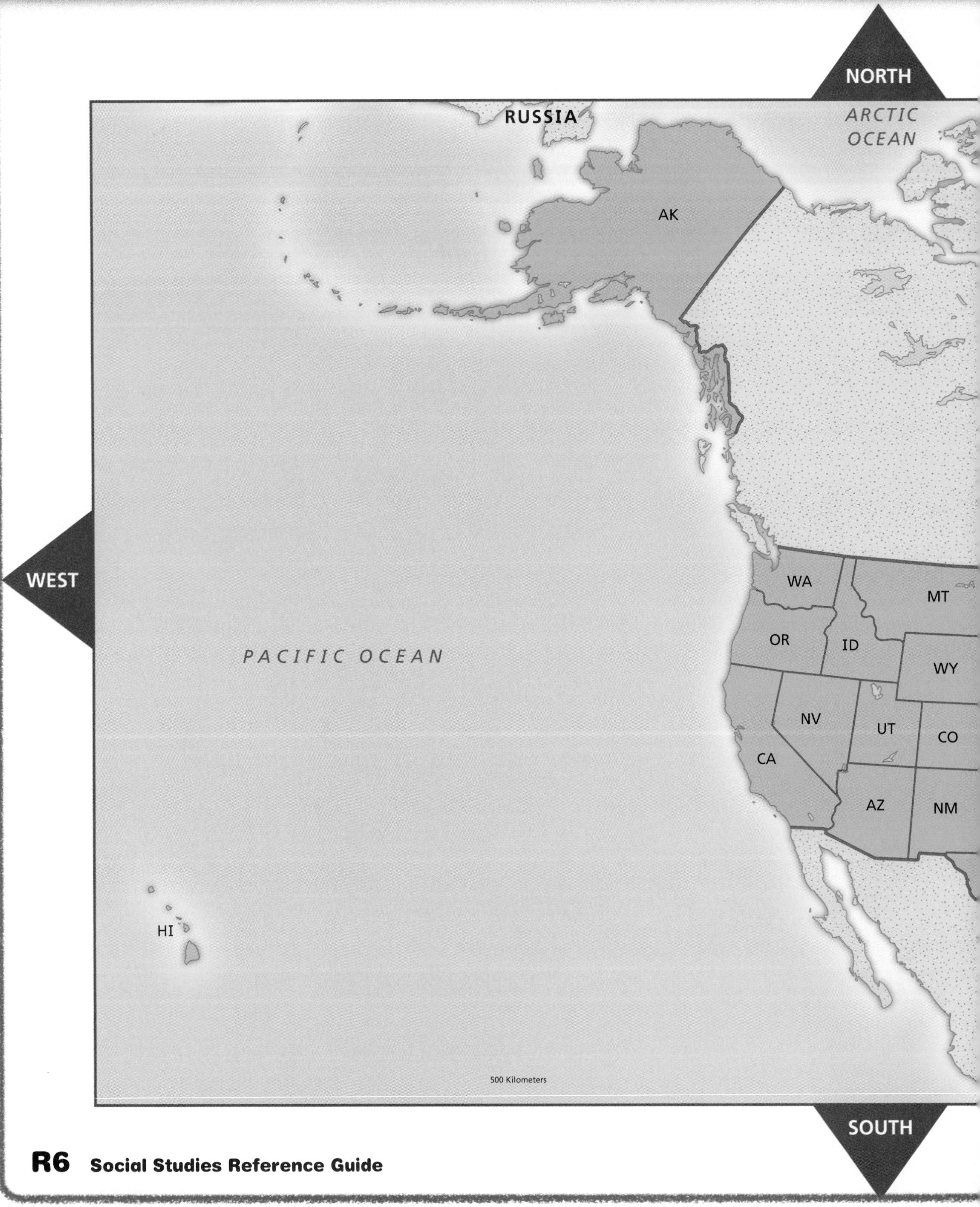
NORTH
WEST
SOUTH
RUSSIA
ARCTIC OCEAN
AK
PACIFIC OCEAN
WA
MT
OR
ID
WY
NV
UT
CO
CA
AZ
NM
HI
500 Kilometers

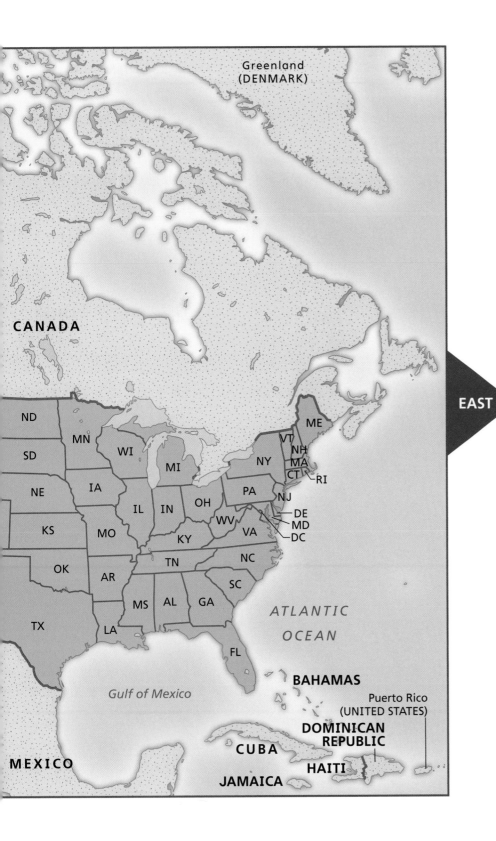

Greenland
(DENMARK)

CANADA

ND

MN

SD

WI

MI

NE

IA

KS

MO

IL

IN

OH

OK

AR

KY

TN

ME

VT

NH

NY

MA

CT

RI

PA

NJ

DE

MD

DC

WV

VA

NC

SC

MS

AL

GA

TX

LA

FL

ATLANTIC

OCEAN

MEXICO

Gulf of Mexico

BAHAMAS

Puerto Rico
(UNITED STATES)

DOMINICAN
REPUBLIC

CUBA

HAITI

JAMAICA

EAST

State or area	Abbreviation
Alabama	AL
Alaska	AK
Arizona	AZ
Arkansas	AR
California	CA
Colorado	CO
Connecticut	CT
Delaware	DE
District of Columbia	DC
Florida	FL
Georgia	GA
Hawaii	HI
Idaho	ID
Illinois	IL
Indiana	IN
Iowa	IA
Kansas	KS
Kentucky	KY
Louisiana	LA
Maine	ME
Maryland	MD
Massachusetts	MA
Michigan	MI
Minnesota	MN
Mississippi	MS
Missouri	MO
Montana	MT
Nebraska	NE
Nevada	NV
New Hampshire	NH
New Jersey	NJ
New Mexico	NM
New York	NY
North Carolina	NC
North Dakota	ND
Ohio	OH
Oklahoma	OK
Oregon	OR
Pennsylvania	PA
Rhode Island	RI
South Carolina	SC
South Dakota	SD
Tennessee	TN
Texas	TX
Utah	UT
Vermont	VT
Virginia	VA
Washington	WA
West Virginia	WV
Wisconsin	WI
Wyoming	WY

WEST

WASHINGTON (WA)

OREGON (OR)

IDAHO (ID)

MONTANA (MT)

NORTH DAKOTA (ND)

SOUTH DAKOTA (SD)

WYOMING (WY)

NEVADA (NV)

UTAH (UT)

COLORADO (CO)

NEBRASKA (NE)

KANSAS (KS)

CALIFORNIA (CA)

ARIZONA (AZ)

NEW MEXICO (NM)

OKLAHOMA (OK)

PACIFIC OCEAN

TEXAS (TX)

MEXICO

RUSSIA

ALASKA (AK)

CANADA

HAWAII (HI)

PACIFIC OCEAN

PACIFIC OCEAN

NORTH

SOUTH

EAST

CANADA

Lake Superior

MINNESOTA
(MN)

WISCONSIN
(WI)

Lake Michigan

MICHIGAN
(MI)

Lake Huron

Lake Ontario

Lake Erie

VERMONT
(VT)

MAINE
(ME)

NEW HAMPSHIRE (NH)

MASSACHUSETTS (MA)

NEW YORK
(NY)

RHODE ISLAND (RI)

CONNECTICUT (CT)

IOWA
(IA)

PENNSYLVANIA
(PA)

NEW JERSEY (NJ)

ILLINOIS
(IL)

INDIANA
(IN)

OHIO
(OH)

DELAWARE (DE)

WEST
VIRGINIA
(WV)

MARYLAND (MD)

DISTRICT OF COLUMBIA (DC)

MISSOURI
(MO)

KENTUCKY
(KY)

VIRGINIA
(VA)

NORTH CAROLINA
(NC)

TENNESSEE
(TN)

ARKANSAS
(AR)

SOUTH
CAROLINA
(SC)

ATLANTIC OCEAN

MISSISSIPPI
(MS)

ALABAMA
(AL)

GEORGIA
(GA)

LOUISIANA
(LA)

FLORIDA
(FL)

Gulf of Mexico

BAHAMAS

CUBA

Geography Terms

forest
large area of land where
many trees grow

hill
rounded land higher than the
land around it

island
land with water all around it

lake
large body of water with land
all or nearly all around it

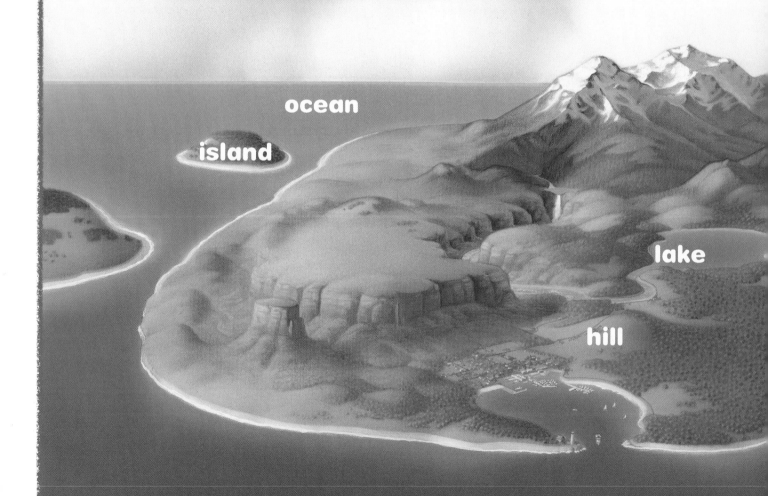

ocean

island

lake

hill

mountain
highest land on Earth

ocean
a very large body of salt water

plain
very large area of flat land

river
large stream of water leading to a lake, another river, or ocean

mountain

plain

river

forest

Picture Glossary

My address is 9 Green Street.

A

address

A way to find a home or another building. My **address** is 9 Green Street. (page 50)

alike

How things are the same. These houses look **alike.** (page 49)

B

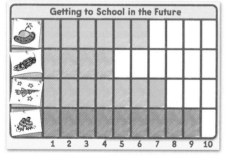

bar graph

A picture that shows how many or how much. This **bar graph** shows how children might get to school in the future. (page 254)

C

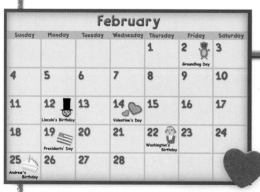

calendar

A chart that shows the days, weeks, and months of the year. I circled Presidents' Day on the **calendar.** (page 20)

capital

The city where important leaders of a state or country live and work. Washington, D.C., is the **capital** of the United States. (page 220)

chart

A way to show things using words and pictures. This **chart** shows the jobs we have at home. (page 98)

citizen

A member of a state and country. I am a **citizen** of the United States of America. (page 218)

city

A big community where many people live and work. My dad works in the **city**. (page 56)

colony

A place that is ruled by a country that is far away. Virginia was once a **colony**. (page 202)

communicate

Give and get information. People can use a telephone to **communicate.** (page 246)

community

A group of people and the place where they live. I live in a big **community** with many neighborhoods. (page 56)

Picture Glossary

continent

A very large piece of land. South America is a **continent.** (page 76)

country

A land where a group of people live. My **country** is the United States of America. (page 16)

custom

The way people usually do something. It is a **custom** in my family to go to a Chinese New Year parade. (page 62)

diagram

A drawing that shows the parts of something. This **diagram** shows the parts of a Native American earth lodge. (page 193)

different

How things are not the same. Many **different** kinds of homes are in my neighborhood. (page 49)

directions

North, south, east and west. The **directions** on a map helped us find the park. (page 60)

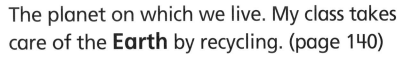

Earth

The planet on which we live. My class takes care of the **Earth** by recycling. (page 140)

endangered

A plant or animal of which very few are living. The mountain gorilla is **endangered.** (page 175)

farm

Land people use to raise crops or animals. My family raises corn on our **farm**. (page 57)

flag

A symbol that stands for a country. The American flag is a **symbol** of our country. (page 16)

freedom

A person's right to make choices. Many people in the United States show flags to celebrate their **freedom**. (page 198)

Picture Glossary

globe

A round model of the earth. A **globe** shows the earth's land and water. (page 154)

goods

Things that are grown or made. A farmer grows **goods** such as fruits and vegetables. (page 108)

group

A number of persons or things. I have a **group** of friends at school. (page 9)

hill

Land that is higher than the land around it. We climbed to the top of the **hill.** (page 151)

history

The story of people and places from the past. I like reading about what people in our country's **history** wore. (page 164)

holiday

A special day. Independence Day is a **holiday.** (page 212)

invention

Something new. The telephone was an important **invention.** (page 246)

inventor

Someone who makes or invents something new. Alexander Graham Bell was a famous **inventor**. (page 247)

job

The work people do. My neighbor's **job** is to paint houses. (page 94)

lake

A large body of water that has land either totally or almost totally around it. A **lake** is smaller than an ocean. (page 152)

Picture Glossary

law

A rule that people must obey. It is a **law** that cars must stop at stop signs. (page 70)

leader

Someone who helps people decide what to do. The **leader** of a community is called a mayor. (page 71)

map

A drawing of a real place. This is a **map** of my neighborhood park. (page 54)

map key

Tells what the symbols on a map mean. Look at the **map key** to help you read the map. (page 55)

market

A place where goods are sold. We buy fruit at the **market**. (page 238)

money

Coins or bills that people use to buy goods. **Money** used in different countries can look different. (page 104)

mountain

The highest kind of land. The **mountain** has snow on the top. (page 150)

natural resource

A useful thing that comes from nature. Water is a **natural resource.** (page 156)

needs

Things people must have to live. Food is one of our **needs.** (page 100)

neighborhood

A place where people live, work, and play. I like the **neighborhood** where I live. (page 52)

ocean

A very large body of salt water. An **ocean** can have many waves. (page 76)

Picture Glossary

plain
A large, mostly flat piece of land. This farm is on a **plain.** (page 151)

President
Our country's leader. The **President** of the United States makes many important decisions. (page 215)

recycle
A process where things can be made into new things. I put many things in our **recycle** bin at home. (page 172)

reduce
To use less of something. I try to **reduce** the amount of paper I use. (page 171)

reuse
To use something again. I will **reuse** this shoe box. (page 171)

river

A long body of water which usually moves toward a lake or the ocean. We traveled down the **river** in a boat. (page 153)

route

A way to get from one place to another. The truck follows a **route** to the store. (page 120)

rule

Something that tells us what to do and what not to do. One **rule** we have at school is to only cross the street with the crossing guard. (page 22)

school

The place where we learn. I take a bus to **school.** (page 6)

service

A job a person does to help others. As a firefighter, my mom provides a **service** to our neighborhood. (page 109)

Picture Glossary

state
A part of a country. Florida is a **state** in our country. (page 75)

symbol
A picture that stands for a real thing. The picture shows a **symbol** for a tree. (page 54)

time line
A chart that shows the order in which things happen. The **time line** shows it will be windy on Wednesday. (page 146)

tools
Things that are used to help people do work. Scissors, a ruler, and a pencil are different kinds of **tools.** (page 108)

town
A small community. Our **town** has many small stores. (page 57)

transportation
A car, bus, or other way that people and goods move from place to place. A school bus is a kind of **transportation** that takes me to school. (page 124)

volunteer

A person who works for free. The **volunteer** helps children cross the street. (page 110)

vote

A choice that gets counted. Citizens of the United States **vote** for a new President every four years. (page 218)

wants

Things we would like to have. Some of my **wants** are presents and cake. (page 101)

weather

How it is outside at a certain place and time. The **weather** is stormy with lightning. (page 142)

world

A name for Earth and everything on it. The picture shows how the **world** looks from space. (page 258)

Index

Index

Credits

Dorling Kindersley (DK) is an international publishing company specializing in the creation of high quality reference content for books, CD-ROMs, online materials, and video. The hallmark of DK content is its unique combination of educational value and strong visual style. This combination allows DK to deliver appealing, accessible, and engaging educational content that delights children, parents, and teachers around the world. Scott Foresman is delighted to have been able to use selected extracts of DK content within this Social Studies program. 66-67 from *Celebrations* by Anabel Kindersley and Barnabas Kindersley. Copyright ©1997 by Dorling Kindersley Limited. 126-127 from *Eye Openers: Trucks* edited by Jane Yorke. Copyright ©1991 by Dorling Kindersley Limited. 194-195: from North American Indian by David Murdoch. Copyright ©2000 by Dorling Kindersley Limited. 250-251 from *Eyewitness: Invention* by Lionel Bender. Copyright ©2000 by Dorling Kindersley Limited.

MAPS: MapQuest.com

ILLUSTRATIONS: H25 Jeff Grunewald 4, 46 Tom Barrett 10, 11 Robert Gunn 17, 90, 138 Susan Simon 20, 32 Keith Batchelor 36 Benrei Huang 54 Donna Catanese 60, 62 Robert Krugle 78 Bradley Clark 80 Susan Tolonen 83 David Brion 84, 157 Steven Boswick 114 Laurie Harden 116 Eileen Mueller Neill 122 Stacey Schuett 155, 190 Amy Vangsgard 176 Richard Stergulz 200 Doug Knutson 206 Ann Barrow 208 Tony Nuccio 216 Bill & Debbie Farnsworth 224 Darryl Ligasan 227 Mark Stein 228 Rose Mary Berlin 266-267 Karen Stormer Brooks H17, H25 Jeff Grunewald EM1 Leland Klanderman

PHOTOGRAPHS: Every effort has been made to secure permission and provide appropriate credit for photographic material. The publisher deeply regrets any omission and pledges to correct errors called to its attention in subsequent editions. Unless otherwise acknowledged, all photographs are the property of Scott Foresman, a division of Pearson Education. Photo locators are denoted as follows: Top (T), Center (C), Bottom (B), Left (L), Right (R), Background (Bkgd).

Front Matter: E1 (TC) ©Joel W. Rogers/Corbis;(TL) ©Robert W. Ginn/PhotoEdit;(C) ©Ed Wargin/Corbis;(CL) ©Joseph De Sciose/Aurora & Quanta Productions;(BC) ©Mark E.Gibson Stock Photography;(BC) ©Lester Lefkowitz/Corbis E2 (L) ©Troy and Mary Parlee/Alamy.com;(R) ©Ron Niebrugge/Alamy.com E3 (BC) ©Marilyn "Angel" Wynn/Nativestock;(CR) ©David Young-Wolff/PhotoEdit;(C) ©Joel W. Rogers/Corbis;(L) ©Dr. Eric Chalker/Index Stock Imagery E4 (BR) ©LWA-Dann Tardif/Corbis;(Bkgd) Bootheel Youth Museum E5 (BR) ©Robert Rathe/Getty Images;(C) Getty Images;(BL) ©Michael Newman/PhotoEdit E6 (BR) ©James A. Sugar/Corbis;(CR) Microstock; (BC) Comstock Inc. E7 (C) NASA/Corbis;(BR) NASA;(BC) ©Robert W. Ginn/PhotoEdit E8 (CR) ©Ed Wargin/Corbis;(CL) Mackinac State Historical Park E9 (TC) ©Macduff Everton/Corbis;(Bkgd) ©Vic Bider/Photri – Microstock; (TL) ©Dave G. Houser/Houserstock, Inc;(CR) Corbis E10 (TL) ©Hal Horwitz/Corbis; (BC) Alamy.com;(TR) Corbis;(TR) ©Lisa Romerein/Botanica;(BCL) ©2002Allan Mandell/Portland Classical Chinese Garden;(Bkgd) Getty Images E11 (TL) ©Dave G. Houser/Houserstock, Inc; (BR) ©Armen Kachaturian/© Comstock Inc; (BC) Portland Classical Chinese Garden; (BL) ©Peter Bowater/Alamy.com E12 (TL) Getty Images; (CL) Bristol Fourth of July Committee; (CL) ©Joseph De Sciose/Aurora & Quanta Productions; (CL)PhotoDisc; (BC) digitalvisiononline.com; (TC,BC) Getty Images E13 (BR) Thinkstock; (TL) Bristol Fourth of July Committee; (CL) ©Tony Freeman/PhotoEdit E14 (C) ©John Elk III/Bruce Coleman Inc.;(L) ©George D. Lepp/Corbis;(Bkgd) ©John Cleare/Alamy.com E15 (BL) ©Mark E. Gibson Stock Photography;(TC) AP/Wide World Photos;(BR) ©Joseph Sohm/The Image Works, Inc;(BR) Corbis E16 (CR) United States Postal Service. Displayed with permission. All rights reserved. Written authorization from the Postal Service is required to use, reproduce, post, transmit, distribute, or publicly display these images; (CL) ©Lester Lefkowitz/Corbis; (TC) ©Joseph Sohm; ChromoSohm Inc./Corbis H2 (C) ©Robert E Daemmrich/Getty Images H4 (TC) ©Warren Morgan/Corbis, (TL) ©Comstock Inc., (TR) ©David Roth/Getty Images, (BR) ©Comstock Inc., (BC) ©Jim Cummins/Getty Images, (BL) ©Mitch York/Getty Images H5 ©Bill Losh/Getty Images H6-H7 Colonial Williamsburg Foundation;(C) ©Robert Glusic/PhotoDisc H8 (TL) ©Eric Meola/Getty Images;(BL) ©James P. Blair/Corbis;(CL) Getty Images H9 (B) ©Ariel Skelley/Masterfile Corporation H10-H11 Colonial Williamsburg Foundation H18 (C) Getty Images H24 (C) ©Charles Shoffner/Index Stock Imagery

Unit 1: 4 (T) Frank Siteman/Index Stock Imagery, (C) David Young-Wolff/PhotoEdit 5 Tom Prettyman/PhotoEdit 8 (BC) ©CMCD/PhotoDisc, (BR) Photodisc, (C) David Young-Wolff/PhotoEdit 9 (Bkgd-L) Mark E. Gibson/Visuals Unlimited 10 ©Colonial Williamsburg Foundation 11 (L) SuperStock, (R) ©Peter McGovern/Little League Baseball Museum 12-13 ©Colonial Williamsburg Foundation 18 (L) ©Corbis-Bettmann, (R) AP/Wide World 19 AP/Wide World 20 © Siede Preis/PhotoDisc 25 (T) Daemmrich Photography, (BR) Bob Daemmrich/Stock Boston, (BL)Getty Images 26, 27 Tony Freeman/PhotoEdit 29 (T) Popperfoto/Archive Photos, (B) Frank Siteman/Index Stock Imagery 30 (B) Jeffry W. Myers/Stock Boston, (T) ©Fox Photos/Hulton Archive/Getty Images 31 (Bkgd) ©PhotoLink/PhotoDisc 33 (T) ©Corbis-Bettmann, (B) ©Corbis 38 (TL) Frank Siteman/Index Stock Imagery, (BL) Tom Prettyman/PhotoEdit 39 (TR) Laura Dwight/PhotoEdit, (BR) Michael Newman/PhotoEdit, (C) Gregg Mancuso/Stock Boston **Unit 2:** 44 Ellis Vener (C) 46 (T) Michael Newman/PhotoEdit, (TC) SuperStock, (B) Mauritius/Robertstock.com, (BC) ©Hisham F. Ibrahim/PhotoDisc 47 (B) ©A & L Sinibaldi/Getty Images 48 (BL) Daemmrich Photography, (BR) Amy C. Etra/PhotoEdit, (T) ©David Buffington/PhotoDisc 49 (BL) Felicia Martinez/PhotoEdit, (BR) Rhoda Sidney/PhotoEdit 50 (T) Daemmrich Photography 52 (B) ©Michael S. Yamashita/Corbis, (T) Michael Newman/PhotoEdit 56 ©Angelo Cavalli/Getty Images 57 (T) Michele Burgess/Stock Boston, (B) ©1997 Chuck Pefley/Stock Boston 57 (C) Getty Images 58 Courtesy of Florida State Archives 59 ©Larry Gatz/Getty Images 64 ©Kevin Fleming/Corbis 66, 67 Barnabas and Anabel Kindersley/©Dorling Kindersley 69 Ohio Historical Society 70 (BL) ©David Hiller/PhotoDisc, (BR) ©Hisham F. Ibrahim/PhotoDisc, (BC) Mark C. Burnett/Stock Boston, (TR) Aneal Vohra/Unicorn Stock Photos 73 (CR) Jane Addams Memorial Collection (JAMC negs. A3.132r1s4), Department of Special Collections, The University Library, University of Illinois at Chicago 74 ©Susan Pierres 79 Courtesy of Florida State Archives (C) ©Bettman/Corbis

Unit 3: 90 (T) ©Bob Daemmrich/Image Works 91 (TC) Spencer Ainsley/Image Works, (BC) ©R. Hutchings/PhotoEdit, (B) ©David Young-Wolff/Getty Images 102 (TL) Bridgeman Art Library International, Ltd., (BL) ©PhotoDisc, (BR) David Young-Wolff/PhotoEdit 103 (TL) ©Siede Preis/PhotoDisc, (BR) Courtesy Action Products International, Inc. 111 (L) Richard Pasley/Stock Boston, (C), (R) Michael Newman/PhotoEdit 112 Courtesy Pam Woolery 117 (T) Runk/Schoenberger/Grant Heilman Photography, (C) Grant Heilman/Grant Heilman Photography, (B) ©David R. Frazier Photolibrary 118 (T) ©David R. Frazier Photolibrary, (C) Grant Heilman/Grant Heilman Photography, (B) Larry Lefever/Grant Heilman Photography 123 (L) Inga Spence/Index Stock Imagery, (R) Hulton Archive/Getty Images 124 (TL), (CL) ©Corbis, (BL) ©PhotoDisc, (BR) Joe Sohm/Image Works 125 (BR) ©Corbis, (B) ©David Young-Wolff/Getty Images, (T) David Young-Wolff/PhotoEdit 126 (C) ©Dorling Kindersley, (B) Stephen Oliver/©Dorling Kindersley, (CL) ©Dave Hopkins 127 (T), (C) Stephen Oliver/©Dorling Kindersley, (TR), (CL), (BR) ©Dave Hopkins **Unit 4:** 136,137 (Bkgd) Lee Rentz/Bruce Coleman Inc. 138 (T) Kent Wood/Photo Researchers, Inc., (C) ©Wolfgang Kaehler, (B) Georg Gerster/Photo Researchers, Inc. 139 (B) Andy Levin/Photo Researchers, Inc., (T) Charlie Ott/Photo Researchers, Inc., (TC) ©Pat O'Hara/Corbis, (BC) ©Robert Glusic/PhotoDisc 141 (C) Bridgeman Art Library International, Ltd., (TR), (BL) Hemera Studio 142 (Bkgd) ©Randy Wells/Getty Images 143 (RBkgd) ©Nick Daly/Getty Images, (LBkgd) ©1989 Joseph Nettis/Stock Boston 148, 149 Smithsonian Institution 150 Lee Rentz/Bruce Coleman Inc. 151 (T) ©Josef Beck/Getty Images, (B) Georg Gerster/Photo Researchers, Inc. 152 ©Patrick Ward/Corbis 153 Myrleen Ferguson Cate/PhotoEdit 156 Michael Gadomski/Animals Animals/Earth Scenes 158 ©Emma Lee/PhotoDisc 159 (T) ©Siede Preis/PhotoDisc 160, 161 Courtesy Tree Musketeers 163 (T) Courtesy Elvia E. Niebla, Ph.D., (B) ©Siede Preis/PhotoDisc 164 www.Living History Farms.org 166 (L) Culver Pictures Inc., (C) Living History Farms, (BR) Michael Gadomski/Animals Animals/Earth Scenes, (Bkgd) ©F. Schussler/PhotoLink/PhotoDisc 169 (B) Obverse ©1999 U.S. Mint. All Rights Reserved. Used with Permission./United States Mint, (T) ©Bettmann/Corbis 174 (T) Tom McHugh/Photo Researchers, Inc., (B) Phillip Colla Photography 175 (T) Lynn M. Stone/Bruce Coleman Inc., (C) E. Hanumantha Rao/Photo Researchers, Inc., (B) ©Joe McDonald/Corbis **Unit 5:** 186 (B) ©Museum of the City of New York/Corbis, (BC) ©Joseph Sohm; ChromoSohm Inc./Corbis, (T) ©David & Peter Turnley/Corbis 187 (C) Bob Daemmrich/Daemmrich Photography, (B) Jeff Greenberg/PhotoEdit 189 ©Bettmann/Corbis 191 Chuck Place/Stock Boston 192 ©Corbis-Bettmann 193 American Museum of Natural History/©Dorling Kindersley 194-195 American Museum of Natural History/©Dorling Kindersley 197 The Granger Collection, New York 198 (T) The Granger Collection, New York 199 ©Bettmann/Corbis 202 ©Francis G. Mayer/Corbis 203 The Granger Collection, New York 204 (C) ©Bettmann/Corbis, (BL) ©Lee Snider/Corbis 205 Stock Montage Inc. 207 (T) ©Bettmann Archive/Corbis, (B) Courtesy of the Historical and Interpretive Collections of the Franklin Institute 208 (R) ©Gail Mooney/Corbis, (BL) ©Bill Ross/Corbis 209 (TL) ©Mark E. Gibson Stock Photography;(BR) ©Grant V. Faint/Getty Images (BL) ©W. Perry Conway/Corbis, (TR) Obverse ©U.S. Mint 211 (T) ©Bob Rowan/Progressive Image/Corbis 212 AP/Wide World 213 (TC) AP/Wide World, (B) Rhoda Sidney/PhotoEdit, (TR) ©Bettmann Archive/Corbis, (TL) ©Benn/Corbis, (CR) ©2000 USPS 214 ©Flip Schulke/Corbis 215 (CR) Stock Montage Inc., (T) ©Museum of the City of New York/Corbis 217 (B) ©Morton Beebe/Corbis, (T) ©Corbis-Bettmann 218 David Young-Wolff/PhotoEdit 220 (CL) ©Ellis Vener;(BC) SuperStock 221 The Granger Collection, New York 222 (R) Courtesy of FDR Library, Hyde Park, NY, (L) AP/Wide World 226 (TL) Library of Congress, (TR) Jeff Greenberg/PhotoEdit, (BL) David Young-Wolff/PhotoEdit, (BR) AP/Wide World **Unit 6:** 231 (Bkgd) ©Joseph Sohm; ChromoSohm Inc/Corbis 232 (Bkgd) ©Lawrence Manning/Corbis 233 (T) ©Adrain Carroll/Corbis 234 (C) SuperStock, (T) Gary Retherford/Photo Researchers, Inc. 235 (B) ©PhotoDisc, (T) © Getty Images 239 (C) ©David Young-Wolff/Stone 240 (BL) The Granger Collection, NY;(BR) Ancient Art & Architecture Collection Ltd. 241 (TL) SuperStock;(TR) The Granger Collection, NY 243 (TL) National Museum of Dentistry, Baltimore, MD, (TCR) SuperStock, (TCL) ©Schenectady Museum; Hall of Electrical History Foundation/Corbis, (TR) ©C Squared Studios/PhotoDisc, (BCL) ©Chase Swift/Corbis, (TC) ©Bettmann/Corbis, (BCR) ©C Squared Studios/PhotoDisc, (BC) ©David Young-Wolff/Getty Images 245 Courtesy of Fulcrum Publishing 247 (BR) Photo Researchers, Inc., (T) The Granger Collection, New York, (BL) North Wind Picture Archives 248 (R) Library of Congress, (L) SuperStock 249 ©Corbis-Bettmann 250 (TL) Ann Ronan Picture Library, (TC), (R), (BL), (BC) Science Museum/©Dorling Kindersley, (CL) Mary Evans Picture Library 251 Science Museum/©Dorling Kindersley 252 (L) North Wind Picture Archives, (R) The Granger Collection, New York 253 (L) ©Hulton Archive/Getty Images, (R) ©Kim Sayer/Corbis 257 (CR) NASA 258 (BC) ©PhotoDisc 259 Barnabas and Anabel Kindersley/©Dorling Kindersley 260, 261 Anabel and Barnabas Kindersley/©Dorling Kindersley 263 The Newbery Medal was named for eighteenth-century British bookseller John Newbery. It is awarded annually by the Association for Library Service to Children, a division of the American Library Association. Permission has been granted/American Library Association 264 (C), (BR) Barnabas and Anabel Kindersley/©Dorling Kindersley, (BL) ©Will & Deni Mcintyre /Photo Researchers, Inc. 265 (C) Barnabas and Anabel Kindersley/©Dorling Kindersley, (B) ©Jason Lauré, (T) ©Todd Gipstein/Corbis **End Matter:** R12 Rhoda Sidney/PhotoEdit R13 (B), (BC) SuperStock, (T) Jeff Greenberg/PhotoEdit, (C) Jim Olive Photography R14 (T) ©Kevin Fleming/Corbis, (C) American Museum of Natural History/©Dorling Kindersley, (BR) Amy C. Etra/PhotoEdit, (BL) ©David Buffington/PhotoDisc R15 (C) ©1997 Chuck Pefley/Stock Boston, (B) ©David & Peter Turnley/Corbis, (T) ©Earth Imaging/Stone, (TC) ©Joe McDonald/Corbis R16 (C) David Young-Wolff/PhotoEdit, (BC) ©Josef Beck/Getty Images, (B) Andy Levin/Photo Researchers, Inc. R17 (T) ©Joseph Sohm; ChromoSohm Inc./Corbis, (C) ©Getty Images, (B) Charlie Ott/Photo Researchers, Inc., (BC) ©Bob Daemmrich/Image Works R18 (T) ©Hisham F. Ibrahim/PhotoDisc, (B) Gary Retherford/Photo Researchers, Inc., (TC) Mauritius/Robertstock.com R19 (BC) Michael Newman/PhotoEdit, (TC) ©Wolfgang Kaehler, (C) ©Pat O'Hara/Corbis, (B) ©A & L Sinibaldi/Stone R20 (T) Georg Gerster/Photo Researchers, Inc., (TC) ©Museum of the City of New York/Corbis R21 (B) Spencer Ainsley/Image Works, (C) Tom Prettyman/PhotoEdit, (BC) Frank Siteman/Index Stock Imagery, (T) ©Pat O'Hara/Corbis R22 (BC) Michele Burgess/Stock Boston, (B) ©David Young-Wolff/Getty Images R23 (TC) Bob Daemmrich/Daemmrich Photography, (BC) Kent Wood/Photo Researchers, Inc., (T) ©R. Hutchings/PhotoEdit, (B) ©PhotoDisc